TONY ALLCOCK'S
BOWLS
SKILLS

Edited by **David Rhys Jones**
Specially commissioned photographs by **Stephen Line**

HAMLYN

I am delighted that Coral Bingo, who are leaders in their field of leisure and entertainment, giving enjoyment to millions of people every year at their Social Clubs, is supporting the game of bowls.

Coral recognise that this popular and fast expanding game is more than just a sport. It is in fact a leisure activity which can be enjoyed by people of all ages and abilities; and like Coral Social Clubs, bowls provides the opportunity to make friends and meet people, and also to have a great deal of fun at the same time.

Tony Allcock

Tony Allcock courtesy McNeil Promotions Limited and TA Services Limited

Acknowledgements
Photographs
All photographs by Stephen Line/International Sports Book Network except the following
All-Sport (UK) 12, 14, 27, 88, 110, 113; Sporting Pictures (UK) Ltd 16, 27, 92 111; Linder Design Associates 90; Eric Whitehead 107

Artwork Mei Lim

Published by
The Hamlyn Publishing Group Limited
a division of the Octopus Publishing Group
Michelin House, 81 Fulham Road
London SW3 6RB
and distributed for them by
Octopus Distribution Services Limited
Rushden, Northamptonshire NN10 9RZ

First published in 1988

ISBN 0 600 55778 2

Printed by Mandarin Offset, Hong Kong

CONTENTS

INTRODUCTION

If bowls isn't the oldest game, surely it must be the most natural, and perhaps the simplest. It can also lay claim to be one of the most sociable, and, I am proud to say, one of the most civilised.

Thousands of people, all over the world, derive great fun and enjoyment from the silly pastime of rolling balls across a lawn at another smaller ball they call the "jack". There is competition, rivalry, and a lot of banter. But most of all there is camaraderie, goodwill and fellowship, and a complete disregard for differences of rank, riches or religion.

That is how it should be in any sport — but heaven knows it is rarely so these days, when spectators and participants seem to rival each other to earn scandalous headlines in the nation's tabloid press. So far, at least, we have had no bottle-throwing in bowls, no ugly scenes on the terraces, and no sad sagas of drug-taking, rabble-rousing or hell-raising — although there has, admittedly, been the odd, all-night party!

Bowlers are not angels — why on earth should they be? But they are, I feel, good ambassadors for sport. It is marvellous to be part of the competitive cut-and-thrust of a keen game, while, at the same time, being able to appreciate — and even enjoy — the skill of your opponent. Thank goodness that bowls still embodies all that is best in sport.

It is especially encouraging, now that bowls has a growing profile on television, that the general public is being introduced to our ancient game. And, from what I hear them say, people seem to like what they see. Part of my aim in this book is to make some of the seemingly more complicated and confusing parts of the game clearer to those who know little about it, but who are interested enough to want to learn.

I hope as well that beginners will find the book useful as they struggle to find a delivery which is suitable for them. Maybe the book will be of value to established and experienced players, anxious to analyse the game, or to improve their performance. I know I have learnt quite a bit about my own game by having to try to appraise it as an objective observer, as it were.

As I will state again and again, I am a natural player, and am proud of it. I have no wish to advocate any particular style, delivery or approach. Neither, I am glad to say, does the official English Bowls Coaching Scheme. My message briefly, will be to keep it natural. But that does not mean we cannot benefit from a bit of technical analysis now and again.

My other hope is that readers will find something of interest within these pages, and that they will continue to derive pleasure and enjoyment from watching *and* playing the game of bowls. Wherever you are in the world, whether you play indoors or out, whether you are socially motivated or competitively inclined, remember that bowls is a recreation, and should at all times be fun — for you *and* for your opponent!

Good bowling!

WOODS OR BOWLS

I have been to Bruce Hensell's factory in Melbourne, Victoria, and have seen Henselites being made. It is fascinating to see the raw material, looking like dirty gravel, being turned into beautiful, highly polished bowls.

Bowls are called woods because they were once made of wood. The word persists as part of the vocabulary of the game even though you will see very few of the original specimens around today. World supplies of lignum vitae, a dense timber indigenous to San Domingo, have virtually run out, and high technology has stepped in with the perfect answer.

Woods are now made of plastic. A resin of phenol formaldehyde powder provides the compound, and the substance is moulded into bowls which are truer and more hard wearing than wood – even tough lignum vitae – ever was. Fortunately, bowlers have continued to use the expression 'wood' for their plastic projectiles, and a piece of bowling heritage is preserved.

Bowls, of course, are not perfect spheres. They are not even symmetrical. It is their eccentric shape that bestows them with the engaging quality of running in an arc. That is what we call bias. And that biassed arc, although it gives the bowler an extra problem to contend with, actually gives him more options, allowing him to roll his wood to places beyond the reach of a ball without bias.

Why the bowl curves

It is not a hidden weight within the bowl that makes it curve. The shape of the bowl means that its centre of gravity is 'off-centre' – fractionally, but enough to pull the bowl to one side, tilt it, and affect its natural inclination to run in a straight line.

Simply, there are two forces acting upon a bowl in play: the forward momentum, bestowed by the bowler on delivery, and the sideways pull, bestowed by the bias. The forward momentum depends on the

Bowls have been manufactured in Glasgow by Thomas Taylor for almost 200 years, although they are now made of synthetic material.

Bias is tested against the master bowl, and each bowl is stamped before leaving the factory.

scale of the initial propulsion, and will be forever decreasing in proportion to the friction applied by the ground it is running over. The forward momentum, then, is variable. The sideways pull of the bias, however, is a constant factor.

So, the faster the bowl travels, the straighter will be its course, because the influence of forward momentum will be greater, proportionately, than that of the constant sideways pull of the bias. And, as the speed of the bowl drops, the influence of the constant sideways pull of the bias will have an ever-increasing proportionate effect, causing the bowl to bend more as it slows down.

Studying the template of a bowl shows how little 'shaping' there has to be before a bowl is given its bias. The difference in profile between one side of a bowl and the other is almost imperceptible to the naked eye. A skilled manufacturer can modify the bias of a bowl by the minutest shaving of one side.

Indeed, if you were blindfolded when someone handed you a wood, I don't think you would be able to say which was the biassed side. Every manufacturer uses the standard means of indicating which side is which. The basic rule of bowls, therefore, is: 'Big ring on the outside; small ring on the inside.'

Hold a bowl, look at it, and you'll see what it means: the side with the smaller disc stays on the inside of the curve. That's something you will need to remember as long as you play bowls. Bowling a 'wrong bias' isn't a crime, but you'll take some ribbing if you do it!

ALLCOCK'S TIP

● *A lot of today's top players change their woods from time to time. Some have several sets, and like to choose what they think is the right set for the right occasion, depending upon whether they are leading or skipping, upon whether the green is fast or slow, upon whether the game is outdoors or indoors. Buying a set of bowls, it seems, is not the once-in-a-lifetime event it used to be!*

HOW TO CHOOSE WOODS

'It's a shame that the only ways to buy a set of bowls are off the shelf of a sports shop or by mail order. The customer has no chance to try out the set before he makes his purchase. Some manufacturers are making the choice a bit easier these days, by putting more information on the boxes, and by giving more choice, particularly where it matters most – in the degree of bias.

Don't rush into a sports shop and buy a set. Talk to some of the better players at your club, and ask their advice. If you can, ask some club members if you can try out their bowls. You will find they are eager to help.'

For a beginner looking for a set of bowls, the choice is bewildering. My first piece of advice is this: if you haven't bought a set of woods already, don't rush into it. Look around until you are happy that you know what you are doing.

After all, a set of woods will last you a lifetime – quite literally. Why make such an important purchase on a whim, before you really know what you are looking for? Perhaps all woods seem much the same to you – but, honestly, they are not. Do shop around. And let me help you.

Sizes of woods

First of all, there are so many sizes. These days the sizes are given numbers, 0 to 7, which refer to the vertical diameter of the bowl, from 4⅝ inches (117mm) to 5⅛ inches (130mm), rising in steps of $\frac{1}{16}$ inch (1.6mm). There are mechanical ways of determining what size bowl you can handle, but I don't trust any of them. A much more natural method is to try them all for comfort, and go for the biggest set you can handle comfortably.

Put the bowl into your hand, spread your fingers naturally, and see if you can turn your hand over without fear of dropping the bowl. If you can, the bowl is not too big, whatever the artificial tests may say. Perhaps it would help if you read my recommendations on grip (on pages 32 and 33) before you go any further.

Weights of woods

Secondly, there are variations in weight to confuse you. The standard weight bowl is produced from a standard 'mix', so, as the bowls move down in size, so the weight drops proportionately. Medium weight and heavyweight bowls are made from a material of a denser mix, so the decrease in size is compensated and the weight more or less maintained.

The standard weight bowl has served us in Britain very well over the years, and there is certainly nothing wrong with it, but many feel happier with a heavier bowl for two reasons: a light bowl will travel further out of the head when hit by a heavy one; and a heavy bowl is more likely to stay put

in the head than a light one on impact.

Heavyweight bowls may not be ideal for the soggy greens we often have to play on in Britain, but there is a lot to be said for them indoors, and on faster outdoor surfaces.

Indoor and outdoor woods

Thirdly, you will be able to choose between indoor and outdoor models. This is the latest development from the manufacturers in a response to the rapid rise of the indoor game. The makers say that bowls behave differently indoors, because carpets are generally faster than grass, and require you to take more green.

The indoor model, though it still conforms to the Master Bowl (the world standard minimum bias), runs straighter than the outdoor model, to 'compensate' for the faster green. 'You can play the same way on an indoor green as you would outdoors', claim the manufacturers. Personally, I think it is more simply a question of whether you prefer straightish or wide-swinging bowls.

Grips on the woods

Fourthly, you will have to decide whether to go for a bowl with grips, or the plain, old-fashioned model. Grips are those dimples in a circular pattern around both sides of the bowl, and are sculptured there after manufacture to match with the position of fingers and thumb to provide a more secure hold.

Some bowlers find these grips invaluable; others can't stand them, and feel they get in the way. It's entirely a matter of personal preference – in no way do the grips affect the running of the bowl, the amount of bias, or the ability to get near the jack.

Different manufacturers

Fifthly, you can choose from a whole range of manufacturers, including several old-established British firms, like Thomas Taylor of Glasgow, who started making bowls in 1796, and the famous Hensell family of Melbourne, Australia, who by 1980 had produced 1,000,000 sets of lawn bowls under the familiar trade name of Henselite.

All the different makes have their own idiosyncrasies, and often it is a case of having the right bowl for the right green. Like a lot of other people, I use Henselite bowls, and, after changing makes and models several times in my career, feel very much at home with my current set.

Cosmetic differences

Finally, you can opt for black or mahogany, with or without emblems, or even have your woods emblazoned with your monogram, so that everyone will know when you have drawn the shot! All these are trivial considerations, of cosmetic value only, though if playing with a brown bowl is going to make you feel more comfortable, go for a brown set!

With all these factors to weigh up and no previous experience of bowls, the beginner can be excused if he or she makes an unwise purchase. If you are a beginner, therefore, hold your horses. Bowlers are always keen to help, and generally love to be asked. They will willingly discuss the subject with you for hours, but what would really help you would be if they let you try their woods for size. That is what you need most of all.

Then, when you have found a set that fits your hand and feels right in your grasp, perhaps you might be allowed to borrow them for a game or two. Only then will you know if they are right for you, and can set about trying to find a similar set in the shops – or send your order to one of the mail order firms that specialise in bowling equipment.

Above: The number of makes, weights, sizes and colours available makes choosing a set very difficult for a beginner.

Far Left: See if you can turn your hand over without fear of dropping the bowl.

Left: The most important thing is for you to feel comfortable holding the bowl.

JACKS, MATS AND ACCESSORIES

If you do not want to make an investment in a set of woods at too early a stage in your bowling career, you can always hire some each time you play if you are playing at a public green, where there is usually an attendant to fit you out with a set. There will also be mats and jacks supplied as a matter of course. Unless you are a crown green bowler, you will never be expected to purchase your own jack.

The jack and mat

The jack is, of course, the target ball – and in the level green game it is much smaller than the woods (about 2¾ inches (70mm) in diameter). It is these days made of the same basic composition substance as the modern bowl, having previously been made of china. Jacks have always been white, until someone had the bright idea, in 1987, of introducing a yellow jack which

looked good on colour television.

Mats mark the position that bowls must be delivered from and protect the green from possible damage from careless foot control. Foot-faulting is defined on page 19. Mats are made of rubber and have to be exactly 24 inches (610mm) long and 14 inches (356mm) wide. They may be black, white or black and white.

Measures

Bowlers are expected to carry chalk at all times for marking touchers (explained later), and the more experienced player can be relied on to have a measure in his pocket in case he is asked to play third (see page 85) or otherwise invited to measure for shot. There will also be a full range of measuring and other implements in the umpire's kit, which bag of tricks remains a wonderful mystery to the novice until he has been playing for at least five years and is invited to 'join the grown-ups'!

Measures can be of the old-fashioned, but very useful, long string type, called the Devon measure, or its equivalent, the Mickey. Then there is the more modern Terry model, the distinctive Prohawk, and the boules-style measure. Then there are the callipers and the feeler gauges, which are operated with such skill by most umpires. The EBUA has seen to it that standards of umpiring have made great strides in the last few years.

And, of course, there is the sonic measure, which has not yet gained the confidence of all the top players and officials, although I would predict that it is only a matter of time before it becomes an accepted part of the bowls scene. Anything that can make hairsplitting decisions easier and more accurate is to be welcomed.

Other accessories include various forms of wax and cream to give a better grip, polishing cloths and chamois leathers for use in the wet or the dry, umbrellas, handwarmers, books on bowls, diaries, and scorecard holders. And if you're playing second – don't forget your pencil!

There are a great number of accessories available for the keen bowler, but you would be wise to wait a while before investing too much in equipment you might find you won't need.

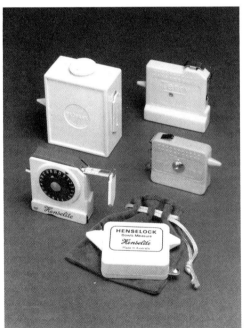

ALLCOCK'S TIP

• My advice to the beginner is again, 'Wait and see!' Don't rush into making purchases you will regret. Ask around, and try what is available. There is an increasing range of accessories, and it is worth biding your time and going for the best buy for you.

BOWLS CLOTHING

❝ Taking advice is even more important when it comes to the choice of bowls clothing. For women, especially, the regulations are still pretty tight, so it would be easy to make a purchase only to find that a particular style, colour, or even material was not officially approved. Ask about greys, whites, blazers, badges and ties – and check on what kind of soles are allowed on your club's green. And be advised by club members before going on that shopping spree! ❞

Bowlers take a pride in their appearance – whites above the waist is a common club rule, and a club blazer will be a necessity if you want to take bowls seriously. Women bowlers look smart in their uniforms, and there are signs that styles are becoming a little more modern.

Far Right: In Britain you must be prepared for all weathers!

The blazer and tie image of the flat green game in Britain has always been a cause of pride. There was always something very civilised about cream flannels and cucumber sandwiches on the village green, whether the game was cricket or bowls, but, although the manners were always impeccable, the turn-out was sometimes a little dowdy, to say the least.

I have noticed a sharpening up of the image over the last few years, and would not be at all surprised to see much more imagination used in the design of bowls wear in the not too distant future, without any relaxing, I hope, in general values and standards.

The influx of so many younger men into the game has had an effect I am sure, as has the television coverage of our sport. The coloured tops worn in the televised events could well set a trend before too long, and why not?

The fashion for white

As things stand, every flat green bowler needs a fairly extensive wardrobe, containing grey trousers as well as white ones. Creams, I am glad to say, have gone out of fashion, and there is much more uniformity in the all-white, no creams approach. Also needed is a white shirt, white pullover, club tie and blazer.

Realistically, no bowler who intends to play outdoors in our summer should be without his waterproof suit, which must also be white. But, ridiculously enough, his bowling shoes must be brown, spoiling the smart image carefully cultivated by wearing all that white.

Recently there has been a strong lobby on the British national associations to allow the wearing of white shoes, but so far they have declined to come into line with the International Bowling Board and most of the IBB's member nations who permit the practice. So, we have become used to the sight of bowlers wearing white shoes on television when they are not allowed to wear them at their club.

Women's clothing

The women's associations have even stricter rules about uniform than the men, and their rules extend to details like the exact placement of the bow on the ever-present hat, and the gloves – when and when not to wear them. There is no doubt that women's teams appear meticulously turned out, although I do wonder sometimes if a few more young girls would be tempted to take up the game if the regulation uniform was a little less matronly.

THE BOWLING GREEN

❝ When you are looking for a club to join, you must consider three things. First, of course, is its location in relation to where you live – that is important. Second is the state of the green – it's much better for an ambitious bowler if he can play and practise on a good green. Third, and in my opinion of great importance, is the sociability of the club – you are going to do much more than just play bowls there, and you will want to enjoy the club atmosphere. When you have found the club you have been looking for, you must hope that they will find room for you – with the increasing popularity of bowls, more and more clubs have long waiting lists. Good luck! **❞**

Having followed the story so far, you are now, in theory anyway, fully kitted out as a bowler. What you need now is a green to play on, outdoors from May to September, and indoors from October to April. What is the difference? Where can you find one? And what will it cost you to play or to join a club?

Let's have a look at an outdoor green first. It is a grass green. Nearly all of them are, although there are a few outdoor greens in England which have synthetic surfaces. Perhaps synthetic turf is the thing of the future, who knows? The green was laid with turfs from Cumberland or Cornwall, or perhaps it was seeded.

The green is a square, with sides between 40 and 44 yards (36.6 to 40.2m) long, is surrounded by a ditch between 2 and 8 inches (50 and 200mm) deep, and is divided into six strips or rinks, each one between 18 and 19 feet (5.5 and 5.8m) wide. Each rink is the playing surface for a game between two players (if it is a game of singles) or between two teams (of pairs, triples, or fours).

The rink
The rink – some 126 feet (38m) long and about 18 feet (5.5m) wide – is bounded at each end by the ditch, and on each side by a thread drawn tightly between a vertical white peg on the bank beyond the ditch. Marking the centre line of the rink, there is another white peg on the bank beyond the ditch. This peg, carrying the number of the rink, is, of course, exactly half way between the left hand and right hand pegs marking the extremities of the rink.

Indoor rinks
Indoors, the surface is likely to be jute, felt or man-made fibre, and, although there are great stadiums in which huge greens of 44 yards (40.2m) square can be laid, many of the indoor centres up and down the country thrive for seven months or more with a modest two- or three-rink green. In Somerset, at the last count, nearly all the 17 clubs with indoor greens have only one or two rinks.

In other areas, like the North East of England, there is a boom in massive eight-rink stadiums, it being possible to fit eight rinks into a green 40 yards (36.6m) wide because the indoor regulations permit rinks to be as narrow as 12 or 13 feet (3.7 or 4.0m) in certain circumstances.

There are around 350 indoor greens in England (35 in Scotland, ten in Wales, three in Ireland) compared with around 2,700 English outdoor clubs. With the great demand for indoor facilities, the management of indoor clubs has to be much more cost effective than that of outdoors. Rink use, because of the demand, has to be regulated very strictly, and leagues, timetables and rotas are everywhere, with rinks never empty.

Unfortunately, as a result, you are unable to get near an indoor rink in the winter for practice. Every game is a league game, inter-club match, club championship or national competition, whereas outdoors it is often possible to book a rink and get in some useful practice. Perhaps the best time of all to experiment with some of the ideas I put forward in this book is in the summer – but indoors, when the carpet is more likely to be available.

Club membership
Most indoor clubs have a long waiting list for membership, while there are still outdoor clubs in some areas that are struggling for members. Bowls, generally, is thriving, and with so many clubs all over the country, there's bound to be one near you if you look hard enough – sometimes they are hidden away in the most unlikely corners, even in busy city centres. There are even a couple of greens, I'm told, in Central Park, New York.

Membership fees – if you can get in – vary from the laughably nominal in some areas that are heavily subsidised by the local authority, to rather more in the expensive and exclusive private clubs. But, even in the up-market clubs, annual membership is unlikely to cost you more than about £60 to £70. Bowls is still a very cheap game to play compared with other sports.

Left: There is something timelessly charming about the typical English outdoor bowling green.

Below: This green at Folkestone is typical of the recent move to take bowls indoors, guaranteeing play even when the weather is bad – and all winter long, too.

THE STANCE

‘I agree 100% with current coaching theory: what is natural is best. Try all the various stances you see being displayed on the green, but be true to what comes naturally to you. If you look all wrong, but your bowl finishes on the jack, who's complaining? I've had enough people criticising my delivery in my time. Now I just don't listen to them.’

No two bowlers ever use the same action. Here are eight examples of the great variety of stances you will see.

I hear it very often said that no two bowlers ever use the same action. That may not be strictly true, for most Australians seem to model themselves on a delivery style advocated by their national coaches, and called 'In the Groove'. Although no centralised coaching has ever been part of the crown green scene, there also exists, it seems to me, a standard delivery adopted by most crown green bowlers. But more of that later.

In Britain, and certainly in England, although coaching is developing strongly, there is a wide diversity of styles, even among the very top players. England's new Director of Coaching, Gwyn John, believes in freedom rather than restriction when it comes to coaching a beginner.

Personal styles

No longer will you hear a coach say: 'This is the way to hold the bowl', or: 'This is the way to stand on the mat'. It is left very much to the individual, with guidance of course, to find a stance, a method and a style which is comfortable, and which may very well be unique to him – or her.

And quite right, too. If I had been 'taught' to play bowls as if it were simply a mechanical matter of technique, I certainly wouldn't have developed the delivery I use – quite effectively – today. I wouldn't have been allowed to, for there is so much about my action which an Aussie coach, for example, would consider to go against the book.

You won't find the Allcock method in any coaching manual, but, come to think of it, you won't find David Bryant's nor Wynne Richards's nor Cliff Simpson's nor Chris Ward's there either. And the man who has contributed most of all to the growth of the English Bowls Coaching Scheme – Jimmy Davidson – had an extraordinary, inimitable delivery, even when, at his peak, he was winning the English singles championships in 1969.

There are so many shapes and sizes among bowlers – remember, in spite of the growing challenge of young players in the game, you don't have to be young and fit to play bowls – that there couldn't possibly be

one delivery to suit them all. Hence the current attitude of wise bowls coaches – if you feel comfortable, it's probably right for you.

Athletic, crouch, semi-crouch, fixed stance, the Scottish runner, the South African clinic, the Bryant style and the Allcock method – which one is the right one for you? Over the next few pages, we'll have a look at them all, and try to analyse what their respective advantages are, but at the end of the day, it's up to you. You may invent a style which beats them all – at least as far as you are concerned.

One thing as least is essential. Indeed it is required by the Laws of the Game. 'A player shall take his stance on the mat' states Law 27. But, apart from a pernickety definition of what constitutes foot faulting (more of that later), there is nothing in the Laws to restrict you to any particular kind of stance.

So use your imagination in your search for a stance which suits your age, fitness and physique, which gives you a sense of balance and control, which is comfortable, but, most of all, which is effective. Try the styles I assess over the next few pages, and then make up your own mind.

Position of feet

'At the moment of delivering the Jack or his bowl, (the player) shall have one foot remaining entirely within the confines of the mat,' decrees Law 27. This allows the player to step off the mat with one foot to complete his delivery – a practice not always observed by the complete novice – as long as the other foot is left behind in a position on or over the mat, 'entirely within the confines'.

It is a good thing to approach the mat – and your position on it – in a businesslike manner. Although I am not going to fall into the trap of dictating how it must be done, I believe firmly in positive thinking, and a purposeful step onto the mat has got to be a good way to start the delivery process.

Most bowlers, except the ones who rely totally on their natural ability, have a check list of actions to go through before delivering the bowl. Why shouldn't the first item on that list be the 'correct' positioning of the feet on the mat?

Pointing the feet

Some regard it as a matter of great importance that the feet should be pointing along the line of delivery (more of that

later) and that forehand and backhand attempts should therefore require quite different arrangements for your feet.

Personally, I don't move my feet a great deal to differentiate between forehand and backhand deliveries, but I must concede that it is basically 'a good idea'. I do vary my position on the mat for other reasons – front to back to add or take off weight, and side to side to affect the line of the swing.

But I would not advise a beginner to try any of those subtle variations: it is far better, at first, to keep the position of your feet on the mat pretty constant, so that

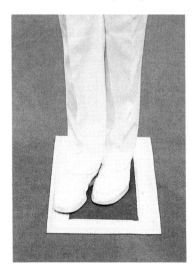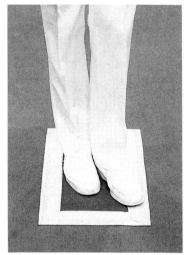

Below Left: Position of the feet on the mat for forehand delivery.

Below: Position of feet on the mat for backhand delivery.

you know exactly where you are. Then you know, at least, that unwanted variations in performance are not the result of sloppy positioning.

Where to stand

Don't stand too near the front edge of the mat, or you will risk footfaulting when your back heel lifts, and your foot, pivoting on the toe, moves clear of the confines of the mat. Don't stand too near the back edge, either, nor to one side or the other.

Stand firmly in a solidly mid-mat position, feet slightly apart, with both feet (if possible) pointing, not in the direction of the jack, but along the line you would like the bowl to roll.

If your feet have a natural inclination to 'tell the time' (whether it is ten to two or a quarter to three!) don't panic. Assuming you are a right-hander, you can try deliberately placing your left (or stepping-out foot) off the mat and to one side, while your right (or back foot) does the direction finding and points along the intended line of delivery.

> ❛ I've seen good players position their feet in all sorts of ways, sometimes with their toes pointing at 90 degrees from their point of aim. If it works for them, good luck to them, but it looks ungainly, and is not to be recommended! Why make something which is quite simple into something complicated? ❜

STANCE: POSITION OF BODY

‘ Quite apart from the *position* of the body prior to delivery, I feel that the *poise* of it is vitally important as well. In 1987, in the Coral Bingo HTV Pro Celebrity event, David Bryant and I were impressed by Suzanne Dando, the gymnast, who had never played bowls before, but has, naturally, great physical control, and poise, together with the ability to relax. If you feel tense as you stand to deliver (as well you might with so much technique to consider) step off the mat, and shake your arms and shoulders. Loosen up. Relax. Then step back on the mat and take up a more positive yet relaxed, concentrated yet flexible stance. ,

Having got your feet into position, the next thing is to get your body into a comfortable and, for you, natural position, poised and controlled yet flexible, relaxed and tense at the same time, odd though that may sound.

Possibly, at this stage, if you are thinking about it too much, you are already beginning to feel wooden and awkward, so it is often a good idea to step off the mat and begin again. Just walk onto the mat and stand naturally, without this time thinking about your feet. That's better! Relax! It's supposed to be fun!

Be natural

If you were asked to throw a stone, or a tennis ball, you would do it naturally, without thought, and without hesitation. It's the same with rolling a ball. It's a natural thing to do. Just do it! That's your natural style. Work on it, and be prepared to modify it if you (or your coach) can spot anything that is creating errors. But don't forsake what is natural to you. I didn't.

The trouble is that very few bowlers can remember what was natural for them at the beginning. Most have had so much good advice from a multitude of well-meaning club members, each of them believing their pet theories to be the definite answer, and all of them contradicting each other. And, now that bowls is on television, even complete beginners come to their first lesson intent on modelling themselves on Bryant or Baker or Bransky, or some other 'B'. It is difficult, therefore, for anyone to be sure if they are really being natural or not.

Perhaps, if you are young and supple, an erect stance is the best for you. Or, if your back or legs aren't as good as they were, you should get the tricky bending over first of all and get into a fixed stance. Perhaps you will aim to make your delivery as economical as possible, cutting out all unnecessary movement which could be the source of errors – not a bad idea.

Or you might try to put together a delivery made up from the best points of the star bowlers you see on television. Terry Sullivan did just that, and became the CIS UK and Embassy World Champion within months. Or, like David Bryant, you can systematically invent and continually modify your very own unique delivery – and look what happened to him!

Listen to advice – but relax and try to enjoy yourself!

Opposite: The athletic stance must be the most natural of all.

STANCE: ATHLETIC

The most natural stance of all must be the erect, upright or athletic stance, favoured by the majority of top bowlers, especially those who started playing bowls at an early age. Only later in life does it occur to us that a swift, fluid stooping movement might involve a little pain and effort

In some ways, too, the high eye level afforded by the athletic stance gives the bowler a better idea of distance, although David Bryant claims that his low crouch actually gives a more helpful indication of line.

If you choose the athletic stance, the extreme version, I suppose, is the ram-rod, but it is not really to be recommended. Standing to attention is not the idea at all. Bowls is too gentle and civilised a game to be played in a military fashion.

Although, in some ways, we are aspiring to achieve something approaching machine-like precision in performance, what we need is a more relaxed approach, with knees slightly bent and shoulders moving forwards towards the line of delivery. There should be some 'give' in the knees, so that the movement when it comes is not too abrupt.

Then, when perfect balance has been achieved, without too much physical effort, the mind can be released to perform its crucial task of concentrating on the matter in hand — for that, quite literally, is where the bowl is!

ALLCOCK'S TIP

● *Although the athletic is the most natural stance, as the name suggests you have to be athletic, or at least reasonably fit, if you are going to adopt it. Most bowlers who took up the game in their youth play from the athletic stance, precisely because it is such a natural way of rolling a ball.*

STANCE: THE CROUCH

❝ Although there is less physical movement involved in the crouch stance than in the athletic, there is a certain amount of leg strain involved, especially in David Bryant's unique version of it. I can't pretend that bowls is not a physical game, however, and I'm sure that most people would get used to the demands of the crouch stance fairly quickly. ❞

The crouch stance is the one most often quoted as the alternative to the popular athletic style, especially for those who are not as young as they were. It involves getting a lot of the movement done at an early stage and cutting down on the physical effort required in propelling a 3½ pound (1.59kg) plastic spheroid 40 yards (36m) or so down a heavy green.

There are several variations of the crouch, but the most common is where the bowler gets himself into a position similar to that of a courtier being knighted by the monarch. From such an attitude of genuflexion, the left foot has only a small step to take, and the arm, hand and wrist movements, too, can be kept at an econo-

mical level, causing minimum strain.

Unlike David Bryant, whose own peculiar, but highly effective crouch (described later) would cause most people difficulties when it came to keeping their balance because of the way in which he keeps his feet close together at first, the more common crouchers take care to form a solid base by keeping their feet comparatively wide apart.

While in this humble position, the croucher can make as many minor adjustments as he wants until he is ready to deliver. Then all he has to do is to time his delivery on the same basis as the athletic style, with everyhting on a much smaller scale and, in theory, under more control.

In the crouch stance, you can get the stooping over with first.

Opposite: The semi crouch is somewhere between the athletic and the crouch – you must find your own version of the crouch stance which is most comfortable for you.

STANCE: THE SEMI CROUCH

Inevitably, there are, between the athletic upright stance and the more contrived crouch, a large range of deliveries that are neither one thing nor another. These offer endless possibilities for experimentation, and you may be lucky enough to find the delivery you have always been looking for.

On the other hand, it is well to remember that your first, natural efforts were probably the best, and that being too self-critical is nearly always counter-productive. Try them all, by all means, and enjoy the exercise, but be sure to stop before you become too confused.

As soon as you incline your body forward and bend your knees to relax the stiffness of the athletic delivery, you have begun to approach the crouch. There are two main variations: the first where you bend your knees more substantially; the second where it is your back that bends.

All considerations of timing, including the step forward and the grounding of the bowl, are basically the same as in the athletic stance, the main advantage of the semi crouch being that, in getting you nearer the ground, movements are minimised and potential for error reduced. The delivery is also likely to be more relaxed, as your knees are flexed and your back is gently bent.

The great danger lies precisely in the 'in-between' nature of the stance. How far is it from either extreme? Is it possible to sense if you are just a little higher (or lower) today than you were yesterday? Some people thrive on such questions, or are so confident of their natural ability that it doesn't seem to bother them at all.

ALLCOCK'S TIP

• *Without realising it, most bowlers probably use a variety of the semi crouch stance. I do so myself. As soon as your knees bend, and you stoop your shoulders towards the line of delivery, you have begun to move some small way away from the athletic and towards the crouch – hence 'semi crouch'.*

STANCE: FIXED

The natural extension of the crouch is the fixed stance, which does away with secondary movement altogether. Get your body into a position where the only thing you have to move is your arm, and you can forget the problems involved in co-ordinating your hand and eye movement with step, body dip and equilibrium.

This is an excellent delivery for those who are stiff of limb, overweight or who have a suspect back, for all the pre-delivery adjustments can be made carefully in advance of the delivery itself.

It is also a good delivery for fast greens, where very little impetus is required. On these the assistance of body weight is not necessary – indeed it could be a real disadvantage. All Australian and New Zealand

The fixed stance does without secondary leg and body movement altogether – very suitable for those who are stiff of limb – and excellent for fast greens.

bowlers I have met have a smooth, controlled delivery that allows their arm to impart the weight of the shot. This is because their greens are so fast that the thrust of body weight into the shot would make fine control very difficult indeed.

Getting into the fixed stance

To find the natural position for the fixed stance, first stand on the mat, gauge then direction of the shot you are playing, the step forward in that direction as if you were going to employ the athletic form of delivery.

Lower your body towards the desired line, and take your stance with most of your weight on your front foot (the left one if you are right-handed). Your hand, holding the bowl, can then be placed on or near the ground alongside your front foot, while your left hand can lend a degree of stability by being placed reassuringly on your left knee.

It is vitally important that you feel comfortably balanced in this position, and that you have freedom of movement for your bowling arm. Then you will be in an excellent position to use your skill, assessing line and length just as you would from the upright, and having all the time in the world to put theory into practice without having to worry about anything else.

STANCE: "SCOTTISH RUNNER"

If the fixed stance has particular advantages for fast greens, there must, at the other end of the scale, be a delivery suited to very heavy surfaces, such as grass greens at the beginning of the season which still have too much grass on them, or greens which have been subjected to heavy rainfall.

Outdoor bowling greens in Scotland, my Scottish friends tell me, are, on average, pretty heavy, and the ones I have come across have been in the 9 to 11 second range (this is explained on page 46), with one or two exceptions like the Abercorn green at Paisley where the 1986 Home International Series was played. Rainfall in Scotland is higher than the national average, so it is not all that surprising, I suppose.

So, it is interesting that many Scots seem to share a style which is diametrically opposed to the fixed stance delivery – for it is a style they have surely come across by 'natural selection', without ever stopping to think it out in coaching terms.

If on fast greens you need no body weight to help you, on heavy greens, it follows, you need lots of it – simply to 'whoof' your projectile to the other end of the green. Thus, many Scots, including my good friend Willie Wood, stand initially in an athletic pose before launching the bowl with their body weight so enthusiastically and wholeheartedly behind it that their own forward momentum carries them off the mat and, with no pause, into a charging run up the green.

Bowls in Britain (not just Scotland) can really sometimes be a battle of strength rather than skill. That is something I regret, and it has led me on occasions to state a frustrated preference for indoor play simply because, more often than not, skill not strength is the deciding factor.

Why, then, does Willie, and a lot more top Scots beside, do so well on fast surfaces? Willie won the Commonwealth Games gold medal in the singles at Brisbane in 1982, and Scotland have done well (though not perhaps quite so well recently) in indoor competitions. That is the $64,000 question!

My theory is that, when they play on quicker greens, these 'Scottish runners', although they seem to employ the same action, do not actually put their body weight into launching the bowl at all. Instead, they 'hover' – there's no better word for it! – with their body weight forward (in 'suspended animation') at the precise moment of release, so that it is their arm, wrist, hand and (especially) fingers that apply the fine control to their beloved guided missile.

If you are inclined to copy Willie and Co, I should point out one potential pitfall. Take care that, in your enthusiasm, your run off the mat does not lead you into the crime of footfaulting. Remember that one foot has to be 'entirely within the confines of the mat' at the point of delivery.

Willie Wood and the 1986 Embassy World Singles Champion, Hugh Duff, run off the mat when they deliver – like a lot of Scottish bowlers.

STANCE: S. AFRICAN CLINIC

The initial step forward is the key to the South African Clinic method advocated by Dr Julius Sergé.

In South Africa they take their bowls very seriously, and are very good at it. Exactly how good it is hard to say, as, since the World Championships of 1976, which were held in Johannesburg, no South Africans, for political reasons, have been allowed to compete in the major world events. Sufficient to say, perhaps, that in 1976, the host nation swept the board, winning Singles, Pairs, Triples and Fours, and of course the Leonard Trophy team championship as well.

Dr Julius Sergé was an influential figure in South African bowls for many years, and

a great thinker about the game. It was he, apparently, who developed a bowling style which is supposed to simplify the process of finding the right line, and the success of the method was first seen in Britain when Bill Moseley won the BBC Jack High tournament at Worthing two years running.

More recently, the figure of Cecil Bransky, an Israeli who learnt to play bowls in South Africa, has become familiar in British televised championships. He, too, uses Dr Sergé's Clinic style, to some extent, as does Welshman, Terry Sullivan, who beat me in the final of the 1984 CIS UK Championship before going on to take the Embassy world title at Coatbridge in 1985.

Although I cannot recommend the delivery as a particularly natural one – it is, after all, contrived for a purpose – it has a lot to commend it: the concept is logical, and it does undoubtedly simplify the process of delivering the bowl along the correct path.

Stand initially with both feet on the mat. Now face the chosen line, and place your back foot (the right one if you're right-handed) so that it is pointing in the direction you want the bowl to travel. That is a fundamental feature or principle of the South African Clinic stylle – the careful positioning of the back foot.

Next, take a short step forward in the line of delivery, with your left foot, just as though you were about to bowl, but keep your weight firmly on your back foot. You may choose to remain fairly upright or bend your trunk towards the path you wish your bowl to take, but it is vital that it is your right foot that is supporting your weight.

From now on, the delivery is similar to that employed from the athletic stance, and of course you are free to use any variations of grip, swing and follow through that will be mentioned in the following pages.

Some people keep their left hand on their left knee throughout the delivery, while others prefer to use that hand to support the bowl at the start, and transfer hand to knee at the natural moment during the action of the delivery itself.

STANCE: CROWN GREEN

I have already mentioned that, though there has been little or no organised coaching, crown green players, and certainly those that I have met, seem to have developed their delivery styles in an uncannily uniform manner.

All the crown green bowlers I know deliver from the upright, and keep themselves more upright than their level green counterparts as they go through with their action. All of them, too, have a very good – I mean smooth – delivery and seem to be very supple and fluid in their all-in-one, straight-backed, swooping movement. Economy of movement is also a hallmark of the typical crown topper.

There are two reasons I can think of to explain the prevalence of the upright stance in crown bowls. Firstly, by standing up, the bowler is giving himself more chance of seeing over the crown – the crown green is so-called because it is shaped like an up-turned saucer, with a crown in the middle (or thereabouts) that may be 18 inches (46cm) or so higher than the perimeter of the green.

Secondly, because they play all over the green, setting at times, if they choose, corner-to-corner marks of up to 60 or 70 yards (55 to 65m) in length, and because crown greens can be pretty heavy, an athletic stance is a prerequisite to reaching the jack at times.

Crown green bowlers are always learning about the line required, as they are forever bowling over fresh grass. So it is natural for the keen crown man to keep his eye on the bowl from the moment it leaves his hand to the time a few seconds later when it homes in, hopefully, on the jack. That is probably the reason for the straight back – giving the bowler a chance to follow the track of his bowl for its entire journey.

Most crown green players are so quick, it often seems to an uninitiated flat green player like me that they are not giving enough thought to what they do. However, the speed of their delivery is also quite easily explained. Firstly, there is little in the way of tactics to stop to think about, and, secondly, if you are finding a touch, it pays to keep on going, rather than break up

Bowling corner to corner on a crown green takes some strength, I can tell you, so it's no wonder that crown green bowlers use the athletic stance, and why they can be seen to be putting their shoulder into their action.

your concentration and rhythm.

There may be much we can learn from the tradition of professionalism in the crown green code – people who play for money learn quickly, and there have been professional players on the crown green circuits for years. As far as their deliveries are concerned, I don't think I've seen a bad one yet!

Most crown green bowlers keep their back foot on the footer (mat) but have a fluid, swooping action.

STANCE: THE ALLCOCK METHOD

'Just as David Bryant's stance is unique to him, and therefore not necessarily to be recommended to the beginner, so my stance, with all its peculiarities, is unique to me. It is not for me to be defensive or apologetic about it – why should I be? I am quite satisfied with my delivery, despite the fact that so many people call it unorthodox. In fact, my basic stance is fairly standard, just a forward lean, and a slight bend of the knees away from the athletic. Then the most contentious bit comes when I follow through – which, people say, I don't! Actually I do, but I'll go into that later.

I have tried most of the other forms of stance and delivery, but I always return to the tried and trusted – the delivery I taught myself when I was little more than a toddler. That's how natural it is, and why, like David Bryant's, it probably wouldn't do for most people. '

My initial stance is basically athletic, but I tend to bend towards the semi crouch – it is the stance which I have found is the most comfortable one for me.

In a way I feel a bit of a fraud writing about my method, because, quite truthfully, I haven't one! Oh yes, of course I suppose I have a method, but it is not a conscious or a studied one. I regard myself as a natural bowler, and have never, until now, stopped to analyse what I do, and certainly never worked on my delivery mechanically like some other successful players do.

Think what a natural thing it is to walk. You never stop to think how you do it. If someone asks you to walk a little faster, you do that quite naturally, too, without working out a method which involves taking a longer stride, or quickening the speed of your step.

But, the technology involved in walking is miraculous. To build a robot, six feet high, weighing twelve stone, with only two small pads called feet that are allowed to touch the ground, and to programme it to balance on those pads, and actually move about without falling over would be a mighty technological achievement.

I have come to realise that my wrist-flicking mannerism is at its height when I am 'on song', and I believe it to be a throwback to my childhood days, when, alone, I would play a 'match' on the lawn, with sixteen bowls, playing all the bowls for both sides. That ingrained in me a fast pace of delivery, and you will notice that, although I may not be a Hurricane Higgins, I don't hang about to this day.

I have learnt that I use a modification of the athletic delivery, making a small concession to the crouch idea by leaning forward into the line of delivery, and steadying myself, from the off, by placing my left hand on my left knee.

I confess I don't pay as much direct attention to line as all the coaches say you should, because I focus on the jack itself when I am on the mat. Although I look towards the line of delivery, it is just a fleeting glance, and my eye returns to the jack – as the desired destination of my draw delivery. I find the line naturally, and without reference to marks on or off the green.

The position of my feet also contradicts coaching theory. Instead of pointing them in the exact direction of the line I am aiming to hit, I tend to move them to a minimal angle off the centre line so that my feet appear to be pointing at the jack. There is very little difference between my forehand and backhand stance.

Where I do conform to the coaching norm is in my step forward, which is 'in line'. I am also orthodox in the fluid transference of my body weight on to my front (left) foot. At the moment of delivery, you will notice that my body and head are quite stable – solid and well balanced, and also 'in line'.

My backswing has a pendulum motion, but my forward swing, which begins as a pendulum, becomes a pushing agent as my forearm, wrist, hand and fingers play their part in impelling the bowl along its path to the jack.

As I will explain later (on page 35), I do have a follow-through, whatever people may say, although it is quite short, and is cut off in its prime by my famous recoiling snatch.

My backswing has a pendulum motion.

I didn't know I flicked my hand away until I saw myself in action on T.V.

STANCE: THE DAVID BRYANT METHOD

' Many people have tried to copy David Bryant's delivery, without success. It is a delivery that has been designed by a technician – a master craftsman – but it is far from natural. That is why it is so difficult to copy. Give it a try and you will immediately see what I mean. It works for David – of course it does – but David is unique! David himself is full of complicated theories about his stance and delivery, and has an unsurpassable playing record to suggest that his theories have at least something in them, but he would be the first to admit that his style is unsuitable for the average beginner. ,

David Bryant's method – the distinctive crouch from which he rises onto his haunches, hovers momentarily, then sweeps gracefully into a perfectly controlled launching action – is as familiar to bowlers and to those members of the general public who follow bowls on the box as his famous trade mark, his pipe.

Few people realise, however, that David's delivery, which he invented himself, is an ongoing piece of work – you could call it his 'life work' – that is even now receiving constant and almost obsessive attention from the master bowler.

You might be forgiven for thinking that, with his incredible record of achievements behind him, David might by now have become complacent, but perhaps it is the secret of his continuing success that he has been able to keep himself 'hungry' for more than 40 years by refusing to become stale or self-satisfied.

Let's have a look at the famous Bryant stance. His crouch is not the easiest to adopt, as the feet are kept quite close together, and balance could be a problem – though not for someone who has been practising it for 40 years!

David claims that starting so close to the ground allows him to assess the required line with great accuracy. That certainly makes sense, for, at the low level, everything appears foreshortened, and the choice of angles is more sharply presented.

· Rising from the crouch, which is what David does next, seems to make the initial crouch unnecessary in some ways, as it could be argued, you might as well start from the upright, or, better still, the semi-crouch, if you are going to return to the semi-crouch position in which David hovers for a second.

Certainly the leverage required to arrive at this point of his delivery must put a great strain on David's back and legs, and would not be practicable for most aspiring bowlers. David must be a very fit man, with great strength in his legs and back developed over so many years of

repeating the same action.

The final part of the Bryant delivery – the descent – is similar to the final part of most orthodox athletic deliveries. It involves the stepping forward with the left foot coinciding with the forward swing and sweet grounding of the bowl, in a co-ordinated and flowing movement, which can only be described as natural timing.

The rotation of David's right arm as it swings forward is not really relevant to a study of his stance as such. I will touch on it in a later chapter. However, consideration of the Bryant method would not be complete without mentioning the separate stance he adopts when he is firing.

The stand-up stance which sends murmurs of expectation around the green at Worthing, or wherever the Clevedon megastar is playing, is not designed merely for effect. Clearly more speed can be generated from an upright position, with a longer backswing and more freedom for body movement.

It helps, as well, to keep your drawing and driving actions in separate compartments, as it were, so that there is no confusion in the hand-and-eye computer. Many bowlers whose drawing and firing stances are the same, seem to lose their touch and their length after firing. David never does.

Bryant's attention to detail is particularly noticeable in the development of his firing stance over the last few years. There is no doubt that he is one of the most accurate drivers in the game. (Remember the final of the Jack High back in 1978 when David was outdrawn by Dick Folkins, an elderly American, but ruthlessly and systematically blasted the Yank's cosy clusters all over Beach House Park?)

For a man so deadly at the drive, David surprisingly is always theorising about the best stance to fire from, and seems rarely satisfied with his current method. One day he will prefer to hitch himself up like a coiled spring, and the next he will prefer a more relaxed, open stance. Whichever method he chooses, he rarely seems to

Left and Below Left: As every bowls watcher knows, David crouches to draw, but stands upright when he is firing.

miss, but that may be simply a matter of confidence, and concentration.

The most important thing to learn from a study of David Bryant is not his technique, which would definitely not suit many of us, but his approach. The way he has applied himself to developing his technique, through total dedication and tireless professionalism (starting long before bowls went professional, incidentally!) is a lesson for us all – though it is a lesson few of us would be single-minded enough to follow.

Above: Although I don't pretend to do it justice, this is my imitation of how David Bryant delivers his bowl.

GRIP

A good tip would be to employ the claw grip on fast greens and the cradle on heavy ones. David Bryant has shown me how his grip becomes more claw-like on faster greens, because he wants his finger tips to have a greater effect on propelling the bowl. There is clearly more 'touch' in the finger tips than there is in the palm of the hand.

Below: The cradle offers no grip at all.

If you were told to pick up a stone in order to throw it, you wouldn't need a lesson in how to do it. The same thing, to some extent, applies to picking up a bowl. There is a natural understanding of throwing and rolling, and kicking as well I suppose, which we have never actually learnt, but which comes to us as part of human nature: instinct, no less.

Even a child does not have to be told about such things as running surfaces, before he works out for himself that a bowl, because of its shape, rolls in a particular way. Beginners understand about bias, even though they may mistakenly imagine that the curve is imparted by a hidden weight or a flick of the wrist.

Some novices make a mistake, it is true, in believing that there should be two different grips, one for the forehand, and one for the backhand. At a very high level, you do sometimes hear talk of tilting a bowl, this way or that, according to which hand you are playing, but to consider that here would be much too complicated, so, for the moment, we will assume that there is one grip sufficient for all occasions.

Position of fingers and thumb

The way in which you first pick up a bowl is very close to the way it should be held in play. Again, nature knows best, and has given you a natural, if impulsive grip. Try it now.

Pick up a bowl, and look at the way your fingers are spread, quite naturally, across it to give security to the grip. Look at the way in which your thumb makes a natural 'C' shape with your index finger, again to lock the grip and hold it steady.

When it comes to holding the bowl 'in anger', as it were, for heaven's sake don't try to contort your fingers and thumb into a grip you have seen prescribed in a textbook – including this one! Go back to that natural grip and use that, subject, where possible, to the recommendations which follow.

The fingers should be (roughly) parallel, and the bowl should be 'straight' in your hand as you extend your palm outwards towards the direction in which you intend to bowl it. The thumb should be used, not as a desperate digit holding the bowl captive, but as a friendly guide, supporting it gently from one side – to stop it falling out of your hand.

The bowl should not be resting inert in the palm of your hand, but should be held firmly, yet gently and sensitively by the fingers, which will be instrumental in sending the missile on its controlled path to the jack.

Finally, your wrist, upon which much of the sensitivity of the whole action depends, should not be stiff and tense – as it probably will be with so much to think of if you're going to get the blasted delivery right. Rather, it should be, like the plastic card, your flexible friend, relaxed and responsive, giving firm and reliable, yet soft and gentle support, to the 3½lb (1600g) weight you are ready to dispatch.

Claw, cradle and compromise grips

In the claw grip, the thumb is held high at the side, and sometimes even over the top of the bowl, while the bowl rests on, or is gripped by, the fingers. No part of the bowl is in contact with the palm.

In the cradle grip, the thumb plays little part in the gripping process as it lies more or less functionless at the side. The fingers, too, are cupping or cradling rather than gripping the bowl.

In the compromise grip, the thumb is playing a part as a 'safety rail', at a point more or less halfway up the side of the bowl, while the fingers are exerting some tactile pressure, although their exact posi-

tion in relation to the bowl may vary according to, for example, the speed of the green – see the chapter on Length, where the effect of thrust from fingers, hand and wrist is analysed.

Advantages and disadvantages

The trouble with the claw grip is that, once it is applied, it is reluctant to let go. Too many beginners grip the bowl too tightly as though they are afraid of losing it. Then they find difficulty in releasing it when the time is right. The calamitous claw grip can often be seen at its worst when a novice is attempting to play with woods which are too small.

The trouble with the cradle grip is that it is, effectively, no grip at all! It is much too easy to lose control of the bowl, causing a nasty wobble, or, indeed lose the bowl altogether, for it has never been properly, literally, in safe hands. This grip is especially lethal in wet conditions.

The advantage of the compromise is that is gives proper tenure of the bowl, without overdoing the grip-of-iron idea. At all times, the bowler feels comfortable, relaxed, yet in complete control. There are plenty of varieties of the compromise grip to choose from, but remember, the comfortable, natural way is likely to be the best for you, even if it goes 'against the book'.

Above: The compromise – comfortable, relaxed, controlled.

Opposite: Spread your fingers, and keep them parallel with the running surface of the bowl, but, above all, hold the bowl naturally and comfortably.

Left: The thumb is held high in the claw.

THE SWING

❛ The backward and subsequent forward swing of the arm is very much like a pendulum, and should be practised until it becomes natural and rhythmic. One top Australian bowler even suggests bowling to music, and encourages his students to count 1–2–3 as they deliver their bowls. ❜

Backswing – swing your arm back as far as you find comfortable.

Having achieved a satisfactory grip, which is firm enough to be secure, and relaxed enough to enable the bowl to be released easily, our next consideration must be the action which is to propel the bowl along the required line to the required distance. And, whichever basic stance you have decided to adopt, it is the movement of the arm which will be responsible for providing the momentum.

We call this movement the Swing, because, pivoted at the shoulder the arm resembles a pendulum, which swings, quite naturally, first backwards then forwards. Some bowlers take this pendulum idea to its logical extreme, letting their bowling arm 'hang loose' and do all the work in the most natural way, although I have seen other bowlers whose arm action could be better described as a push or a shovel.

My own action is not as free a pendulum swing as many bowlers employ, as I tend to impel my arm forward forcibly and deliberately to impart the correct weight. To

be quite honest, I don't know exactly why – or how – I do it . . . but it seems to work! But if you look at my delivery closely, I am sure that you will see the basic pendulum action at work, boosted by a late forward thrust.

The backswing

Some bowlers defy convention completely, refusing to accept the need for a backswing at all, and generating enough power with a sudden forward lunge from a stationary position with the bowl at ground level, normally using a full crouch stance. Although he was slightly before my time, I am told that the great old Welsh international, Fred Thomas, was a splendid example. George Murdoch, of Bristol, who earned many English trials, was another.

The backswing, however, is a feature common to almost all delivery styles, and the most important thing to remember is to allow the course it takes to be unrestricted. Some bowlers slide their hips to one side to ensure this, and David Bryant has his own theory about rotating his lower arm to facilitate the natural and unfettered swing.

The scale of the swing can take the arm just past the vertical, or, indeed, as far back as you like, as long as you are not in danger of inducing strain – which would be first felt in the shoulder – or running the risk of losing the bowl from your grasp. The length of the backswing is one of the factors contributing to control of weight, and I shall be dealing with that interesting subject on page 48.

The forward swing

After the backswing comes the forward swing, which should also be unhampered. If a step forward (from the athletic stance, for example) is part of your delivery, the swing and the step must be synchronised, or at least co-ordinated, so that the bowl may be released from the fingers at the correct split second.

It is, unfortunately, impossible to define exactly when that split second occurs, except to say you can spot immediately when you have got it wrong. If that sounds like a cop-out, I'm sorry, but some things, at the end of the day, have to be left to natural ability!

In fact, to be a bit more technical about it, you can actually vary the timing of step with swing, and this can be a great help when coping with extreme speeds of green. For further details of how the swing can be delayed until the step is completed as a means of 'holding back' on ultra fast surfaces, turn to page 25.

Follow through

All ball games, it seems, have one bit of technique in common: the follow through. Strange as it may seem, whatever has gone on before the ball has gone, however correct the approach and the contact, the success of the action, whether it be hitting, kicking, cueing, throwing or rolling, depends in the end on the follow through.

You might think that once the ball has gone, nothing can be done to affect its travel – and I suppose that, strictly speaking, logically, that must be the case. But the truth is that the performance of a perfect follow through is a kind of post-delivery guarantee that what has gone before has been properly and thoroughly performed.

I know that many will be quick to respond by referring to my own delivery. 'How can Tony Allcock advocate a good follow through when he hasn't got one himself?' I can hear them asking. But I have news for them. I *do* have a follow through, and a perfectly good one at that, although I do admit that, once the bowl has left my hand, everything happens so quickly that it must appear to spectators that I have withdrawn my right arm and hand before I have properly completed my delivery.

I assure you that, although my follow through is a short one, it does happen, and that, before I snatch my hand away, it is an important factor in finding a consistently good line, which people have been kind enough to say is one of my strengths. All the same, I would not recommend others to copy my style, as I am sure a longer, more exaggerated follow through is a more reliable proposition.

It's a bit like looking in the mirror when you are taking your driving test. Not only have you to do it, but you must make sure the examiner sees you doing it. An exaggerated follow through is not only a guarantee of what has gone before, it is a

guarantee to you that you *have* followed through.

The follow through is a natural extension of the forward swing, and should continue the line exactly, with your right hand finishing up, palm outstretched towards your point of aim, about which we will learn more on pages 38 to 45.

'When is the right moment to let go of the bowl? In a delivery which lasts, say a second and a half, the point at which the bowl is dispatched is but a split second. It is clear, then, that the fine timing of this action is critical, but no-one has ever made a proper scientific study of the mechanics of grounding a bowl.

It's not something we should think about at all really – it's another of those natural skills which everyone, to some extent, is instinctively blessed with.

Only if something is going radically wrong with your timing, resulting in premature or belated grounding, and a bumpy launch, should you seek advice, preferably from a coach, who will probably be able to spot quite quickly what is going wrong.'

Above: Forward swing – a natural pendulum.

Left: The perfect follow through is a sort of guarantee of good direction – and looks good, too!

PUTTING IT ALL TOGETHER

1 – 7 From initial
stance to moment of
delivery, your delivery
should look good and
feel good. Feet, step,
stance, grip, swing
and follow through
should combine in
one smooth, rhythmic
action. Practise it until
it is grooved.

It is time now to take stock of the varied options I have presented, and time to try to put stance and delivery together, showing that all the parts – feet, step, stance, grip and swing can combine to make a pretty effective whole.

In the photographic sequence I have demonstrated my own delivery because I have faith in it, and because it lives up to my insistence that everyone must go for what is natural for them – and my delivery, though unorthodox, is certainly natural for me!

The one thing I have modified for the

pictures, simply for the sake of clarity, is the follow through, which, as I have explained, in my case is so brief as to be easily missed. I advocate something more elaborate for the beginner, and I have tried to demonstrate a more orthodox version, even though I have no intention of changing my own style.

The sequence
Pick up a bowl – one you have chosen with care and have confidence in – and handle it as though you are in charge, but with a certain tenderness at the same time.

Caress it in your grip, and arrange it in your hand so that the smaller disc of the bias is correctly aligned for the forehand or the backhand as required.

Stand purposefully on the mat, placing your feet firmly in a central position, but pointing in the appropriate direction, and take your chosen stance, ensuring that you are comfortable, well balanced, and in complete control of the situation. Check your grip, ensuring that it, too, is comfortable, and that your fingers are spread in support and also pointing in the direction of delivery.

You can 'feel' the bowl with your fingers, and your thumb is providing that valuable side support. Your wrist is relaxed without being limp, and you can check the weight of the bowl by jiggling it up and down once or twice.

When you are ready, having mentally assessed the line and length required, time your backswing to coincide with the first-forward movement of your left leg as it begins to step forward.

Then with your hand on your left knee, give yourself a solid platform for the transference of your body weight almost entirely on to your left foot, as your graceful forward swing brings the bowl to the point of delivery.

The release

As you release the bowl you should feel it leave your fingers, but should hardly be aware that it has gone as you continue your elegant delivery to its balletic conclusion in an extended follow through, still perfectly balanced and in control.

If the delivery feels good, it will probably look good as well, and if it looks good, the chances are that it will do you good, and repay you handsomely for your efforts with a bowl nestling cosily next to the jack.

This book is a step by step guide, and it is important that we analyse the components of a good delivery before we put them all together. Therein lies the problem, for, when we try to put the components together we might just forget to include a vital part of the whole action. Be patient. Go through it all again. It is important that you work thoroughly towards the complete delivery.

3

4

6

7

LINE: HOW TO FIND IT

‘In New Zealand for World Bowls, in February, 1988, I changed my attitude to the use of marks to assist in line assessment. The greens in Auckland were so fast and swingy that I was unable to rely on my natural orientation method, and was forced to look for some guidance from marks on the bank.

I realise that the greens we played on at the Henderson Centre were not all that fast by Kiwi standards, but they were faster than those we encounter in Britain, so there was a wider angle between the centre line of the rink and the line along which it was necessary to deliver the bowl than we would ever come across on our greens. ⸮

There are three things, they say, that are important in bowls, and they all begin with the same letter: line, length and luck. The last 'L' is a fickle commodity, and has no place in a coaching manual; the middle 'L' is very much a matter of 'touch', and is difficult to pin down; but the first 'L' is simple to understand and straightforward to explain even though it may often frustrate those seeking to master it.

Line is simply the curving path of the bowl as it makes its way across the green to the jack. Without wanting to confuse the beginner, I should point out that bowlers sometimes use other expressions when they are referring to line: grass, green, land, width, draw, direction and arc are just some of them.

The obvious thing to remember is that the line to the jack is a curved line, an irregular curve which increases in angle as the speed (forward momentum) of the bowl drops and the relative influence of the bias (sideways pull) becomes greater.

So bowling the bowl (or wood) at the jack will result in a visit to the next rink and the plaintive request: 'Can we have our ball back please?' Not a good idea. The line, then, must set off from the mat at a distinct angle to the straight line between the mat and jack - the centre line of the rink.

First, you must calculate that angle with some degree of accuracy (more about this later). Then I suggest you forget, if you can, that the bowl is biassed, and simply roll it along the 'straight' line of your choice (at the right speed of course, and having checked that the small disc is on the correct side of the bowl!) It is helpful to rid yourself of the idea that you are imparting the bias to the bowl. It will do that for itself after it is beyond your control.

Forehand and backhand

When you roll it along a line to the right of the jack, you must ensure that the bias side of the bowl (the small disc) is on the

Right: Forehand.
Far Right: Backhand.

left, so that it will pull the bowl towards the jack. This, for the right-handed player at least, is called the forehand. Rolling the bowl to the left, with the small disc on the right, is called the backhand.

There is no real difference in stance between the two. Whether you are playing on the forehand or on the backhand, you simply roll a bowl in a straight line and let the bias do the rest! If you ask for proof of this theory, I suggest that if you were blindfolded, you would not know which hand you were playing but, if someone pointed you in the right direction, you would bowl along the right line.

Try, therefore, never to fall into the trap of making a false distinction between forehand and backhand, for those who do are basing their attitude on the feeling that they are responsible in some way for making the bowl bend. That responsibility belongs firmly to the manufacturer!

How to find the line

Every green you play on will be different. Even the same green will change, according to the weather and the level of industry of the greenkeeper. Look out for subtle – and sometimes not-so-subtle – changes in pace and swing even during the course of one game. This is true also indoors – the thermostats controlling the heating and ventilation, the humidity and, in my own experience, the intense heat of the television lights can cause tremendous variations in the behaviour of a carpet of man-made fibre.

So, the identification of the correct line to play is not really as simple as it sounds. It calls for acute powers of observation, and for continuing vigilance once the initial assessment has been made. But the main question is how to make that first, quick assessment.

The trial ends, of course, are intended to give the opportunity of reading the green, casing the joint, or, quite literally, gauging the lie of the land. Watch out for a simple contrast between a swinging hand and a 'straight' one, and for any quirks that show up in the behaviour of your bowl. Watch closely, and do not allow yourself to be distracted by hearty greetings or introductions, or by the bonhomie of your opponents.

The use of marks

When you are playing on a strange green, it is a good idea to use the pegs marking the

Lots of bowlers use landmarks to help them find the correct line. The giant ashtray or the chairs on the bank in this picture could assist – until someone moves them.

boundaries of the rink as a general guide, and bowl straight at them. More often than not you won't be far away, but, in any case, you will soon learn from your mistakes. Indoors and on faster outdoor greens, of course, the average swing will be greater than this, and you will be aiming at, perhaps, the centre marker of the next rink.

Personally, I don't use any artificial marks or signposts to help me find my line, but I know lots of bowlers do, and I wouldn't knock it. Some use marks on the green, some use features on the bank, some even use landmarks in the middle or long distance or on the horizon.

I prefer to trust my instinct, employing what I have heard the experts call 'natural orientation', but it is always good to have a technical safety net to fall back on if your natural ability lets you down, so do try any methods you can to fix a line and help you bowl to it.

When you are sure where the line is, and have established guidemarks for locating it, the really difficult bit begins. Now you have to deliver your bowl along the line, putting your theory into practice. The hints on the following pages will help you achieve this.

LINE: THE FEET AND BODY

❝ Although I don't always do it myself, I recommend the practice of setting your feet – particularly the right foot if you are a right-hander – in direct line with the direction in which you want the bowl to set off. This is the base from which you set a solid, properly aligned delivery. The feet provide the foundation for the whole stance. ❞

Right: Make sure your right foot is pointing along the line you want the bowl to take – your left foot initially is not so important.

Above Right: Face line of delivery so that your whole body is ready to move in that direction.

One of the most common faults among beginners is their tendency to stand facing the jack rather than the direction of delivery – or line. It is an understandable error to pay attention to the jack. After all, that little white ball is what the game of bowls is all about.

Once the idea has been accepted that 'green' has to be taken, it should become standard practice to face the line of delivery adopting whatever stance has been chosen. And, obviously, the essential ingredient in establishing a stance has to be the position of the feet.

The position of the right foot (for the right-hander) is thought to be of greater significance at the initial stage of setting the stance, for it is that foot that confers the continuity to the delivery – it is still, in most cases, in position, albeit cranked forward with the heel off the ground but with the toe still in contact, when the delivery is complete.

The left foot, as suggested on page 19,

can even be off the mat and to the side at first, but will normally be parallel with the right foot. The important role of the left foot comes when it steps forward. It is vitally important that the step forward is precisely in the line of delivery – if you like, you can rehearse this step until you are sure you've got it right.

Once the feet are correctly placed as a matter of habit, the whole business of rolling the bowl along the actual line you have selected becomes much more straightforward. There is nothing more frustrating than to be confident that you are selecting the right line only to miss it in practice.

Body position

With your feet in position, it should be a simple matter to get your body in the right place. Particularly where the athletic stance is being used, and the feet are parallel and side by side, there is only one comfortable position for the trunk, and that is set firmly above the weight-carrying legs, and at right angles, as it were, to the line of delivery.

Whether it is the fully upright or the partially crouched athletic stance that is being used, the body should still be in direct relationship to the line of delivery, both at the stationary stage before the action commences, and during any forward movement of the trunk once the process of delivery has begun.

The only exception to this general rule is the sideways swing of the hips that a lot of players seem to find necessary to make room for their arm as it pendulums backwards and forwards.

Keep your eye on the line you want your bowl to take. Pay attention first to the position of the jack to give you an idea of length, but finally concentrate your gaze on the line along which you will launch your bowl.

❝ Don't stand stiffly, or think too much about your body position. Be natural. Stand naturally, facing the line of delivery, almost as if you were talking to someone. Remember the paradox: stand with a dynamic tension about your posture, yet, at the same time, be relaxed, and flexible.

Keep in your mind the goalkeeper, about to face a penalty kick; alert, tense, excited, coiled like a spring, yet relaxed, free to move, fluid, almost serene! That is how you should be poised on the mat prior to delivery. ❞

LINE: HAND AND EYE

❛I remember playing in a tournament in Skegness when I was a teenager, and watching one of the most successful bowlers actually closing one eye, almost like Nelson, when he delivered his bowl. I don't recommend the practice, but it indicated to me just how important that old boy considered lining up his eye with the line of delivery.❜

Right: Hold your arm extended along the line of delivery.

The eye itself is often forgotten when the intricacies of hand and eye co-ordination are considered, but, when you think of it, it is clearly one (or two!) of the leading characters in this particular drama. It is the eye, of course, which identifies the correct line in the first place, and keeps the whole system aware of the spatial relationships throughout the process of delivery.

And when it comes to executing the movements programmed into the body's nervous system on the basis of evidence provided by the eyes, it is the eyes again which unblinkingly and reliably monitor the body's actions.

But is it eye singular, or eyes plural? Most people, we are told, have one eye which is dominant – which undertakes the lion's share, if you like, and upon which they depend more strongly.

Two eyes are an advantage, for sure, when it comes to judging distance, but as far as line is concerned, one of our eyes is more influential than the other. So the

dominant eye is the one we should be placing in or over the line of delivery.

And although we can permit an occasional crafty sideways glance at the jack to remind ourselves of the length, our powers of visual (and mental) concentration should be firmly fixed on the straight track from the mat to the shoulder of the arc where the bowl, we know, will start to turn.

The arm, wrist, hand and fingers

When David Bryant drives, his arm is raised high and outstretched towards his target. He is clearly using his arm as a kind of gun sight before firing, and the steady, unblinking concentration can be seen in the ruthless glint in his eye.

Some bowlers use their arm in this way when they are drawing, and I can understand why they do it. They are sighting their line, and it helps for their arm, wrist, hand and fingers to form a straight line parallel to all the other straight lines being drawn by feet, eyes and mind, and all of them leading to the shoulder of the arc.

Even in less extreme deliveries, the disposition of the arm, wrist, hand, and fingers should be lined up with the desired direction of travel for the bowl. If everything is lined up in the same direction and the movements follow suit, it should be impossible for the bowl to behave in a contradictory fashion.

ALLCOCK'S TIP

● *Some bowlers hold the bowl high, just in front of their face, when they are sighting the line. That is exactly what they are doing – using their arm, and their fingers as an extension of their arm, just like a gun sight, and peering over the top at the shoulder of the arc. As long as the process does not induce too extreme a backswing, I would go along with it – it's not a bad idea!*

LINE: THE SWING

Naturally, after setting up your stance so that all lines are effectively running parallel with the desired grass line, it would be a disaster if, as soon as movement were introduced, the linear objective should be sabotaged. So it is vital that the swing – both backward and forward, should follow the true line.

Playing across the line in cricket is a hazardous business, and results in many an unintentional error and unnecessary dismissal. Wavering from the straight and narrow in bowls produces equally disastrous results.

Hooking is probably the commonest fault arising from lack of attention to line during the operation of the forward swing, while a straying backswing can produce a scooping delivery which tends to produce a wobble or a wide.

There is little you can do on your own to check your swing, though I have seen keen bowlers using a full length mirror, risking charges of vanity. Of course, you could ask the club coach to have a look at your swing, like they do in golf, for more and more clubs now boast a qualified man or woman who can give good advice to novices and to champions.

Better still, you could use modern technology and have someone point a video camera at you, and analyse the pictures at your leisure. Bowls is moving into a new age, and we can expect bowlers of the future to use whatever gadgetry is available.

'With your feet correctly placed, and your grip and arm position carefully lined up, everything should be ready for a well aligned backswing, which should, in turn, give way, pendulum-fashion, to a straight return forward swing. If you are properly relaxed, the pendulum motion itself should guarantee that the swing has no wavering, but, if you are tense, or over-careful, or simply too self-conscious about the movement, you could suffer some sideways shift, hooking or pulling the swing out of its true and intended line. Again the advice is 'Be relaxed – and natural'. '

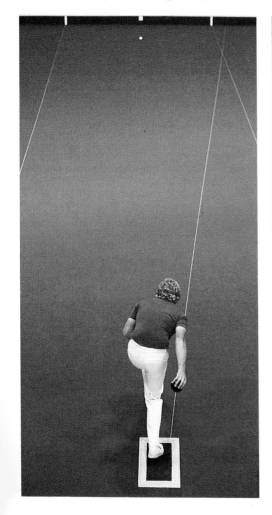

Far Left: Your backswing should be perfectly in line throughout its travel. Avoid introducing any off-line flourishes or diversions.

Left: Keep your forward swing in line – no swerving!

LINE: THE STEP AND FOLLOW THROUGH

‘ Don't be afraid to look good when you are executing your follow through. Think how David Bryant, especially when he is on song, follows through so gracefully that, as he is reaching for the sky with his bowling arm, his right foot leaves the ground, and his right leg becomes airborne. He is left in a position of perfect balance, with is right foot somewhere above his head – like a ballet dancer. He couldn't care less if people smile. Why should he? Why should you? ,

A good follow through looks good, gives a 'seal of approval' to your delivery, and helps to maintain your control of line.

While all the hints for finding a good line so far discussed are important, perhaps the step-through is the most important of all. Assuming that you have placed your feet in a good position in the first place, the step forward is the most drastic alteration you have to make to the shape of your stance, and it is at this point, therefore, that, if you are not careful, it could all go wrong.

Certainly most of the errors in line-finding I notice can be put down to a careless step forward which throws the bowler off balance momentarily, and denies him the control he needs for accurate placement of the bowl on the right track.

The step should be neither too short nor too long – although as I will explain on page 49, varying the length of the step can assist in adjusting to greens of extreme pace, be they very fast or very slow.

Most of all, however, the step MUST BE IN LINE. If it is, and if everything else is as well, the bowl has no alternative but to go in the right direction. Then, all you're looking for is a comfortable delivery with good timing and a smooth release, and you are really in business, and can turn to the pages dealing with length for the final piece of the jigsaw.

Changing your stance

If the step forward in your case gives cause for concern, why not try the fixed stance, as described on page 24, or the South African Clinic style, on page 26. The fixed stance allows you to make the step forward deliberately, after due consideration, rather than relying on natural co-ordinated body movement.

The South African Clinic does not go quite so far, but, while it does not abolish the fluid step, it goes some way to facilitate the correct positioning of the left foot, before the delivery gets under way, and could be of great advantage to those who are hesitant or uncertain or simply erratic in their leg control.

If you stick with the athletic delivery, you can still 'preview' the step forward as part of the routine preparation while standing on the mat. Give a practice step forward to get an idea of where your foot will land. In a way, the step should be as natural as going for a walk (not a march), but there is no reason why you can't develop a 'natural' habit through practice.

The follow through

Assuming that all that has gone before in preparation for the delivery has conformed to my recommendations and you have been able to keep all your actions in line, all you need to do now, as a kind of gold seal of approval, is to follow through in a straight line and you have executed the perfect delivery.

The proof of the pudding, though, must be in performance, and you will be able to judge your success by noting where the bowl has finished.

Don't be too hard on yourself, or the method, however, if you have failed to draw a dead length toucher first time, as there may well be explanations for that which attach no blame to the application of the 'straight line' technique.

Firstly, with so much artifical concentration on getting everything right, it would not be surprising if your delivery had lost all of its natural spontaneity. Relax. Try again, and again, until the movements you are learning become second nature. If you have already been bowling for some time, it is extremely difficult to unlearn your habits and take on another action without a struggle.

Another explanation for failure, if your criterion is the proximity of your bowl to the jack, is that you have misjudged the line you needed to take. It is quite possible that you have delivered the bowl perfectly, along the precise line you chose, but you simply chose the wrong line!

The important thing to remember when executing your follow through is to send your hand after your bowl. If you are using marks on the green, or beyond, that means pushing, stroking or floating your hand towards the object which is your chosen landmark – the bench, hedge, tree, church tower, or distant chimney.

Beware, incidentally, those mobile marks which are sometimes available on the bank – a foot, a duster, or your opponent's wife's handbag. Such seemingly helpful objects can disappear at a moment's notice – or, worse still, be moved without warning and without you noticing. Treacherous!

ALLCOCK'S TIP

● *I have seen players concentrate commendably on getting the right line by taking a careful considered step forward. In doing so they sadly over-stepped, lost their balance – and, of course, lost control. They were obviously thinking so much about the step forward, that they exaggerated that single feature of their delivery. Disastrous.*

The answer? – I'm afraid it's the one I've given several times already: Relax. Don't be wooden, or unnatural in your approach. Step forward as if you were going for a gentle walk, a stroll, not a route march or the second leg of a hop, skip and jump event!

The step forward is perhaps the most important factor in finding line. Make sure, whatever the starting position of your left foot, that you are stepping in line, or you will ruin your delivery at the very last moment.

LENGTH: HOW TO ESTIMATE IT

If line is easily explained and coached, the second 'L', length, certainly is not. Admittedly you could say that length is the distance of the jack from the mat, but that is too simple to be helpful. What the prospective player needs to know is how to get his bowl to stop at a given distance on the particular green he currently finds himself on.

Other words for length include speed, pace, impetus, momentum, 'powder', strength, and, most commonly, weight. And all those mean the 'oomph' that the bowler has to put behind his delivery if the bowl is to travel the correct distance. First, the pace of the green has to be assessed.

Pace of the green

That, of course, introduces the variables that make the game of bowls so interesting, challenging, and sometimes so frustrating. For the pace of the green, which is the factor that governs the strength of the shot, can vary between eight or nine seconds on a British outdoor green in April to as much as 28 or 29 seconds on the equivalent New Zealand green in their summer season.

The timing of bowling greens that produces such diverse statistics is carried out with a stop watch, and involves clocking the bowl's travel over 30 yards. And before we go any further, I will have to stop and explain why, on a very fast green it takes a lot longer for the bowl to travel 30 yards than it does on a heavy (or slow) green.

The key to what seems a nonsensical statement is that the bowl is not timed over its *first* 30 yards, but over 30 yards, on a delivery which has only enough strength to carry the bowl that distance *exactly*.

So, the fast green – that is the one at the height of summer, which has been cut down, rolled flat and baked hard until it shines, and plays 'like glass' – requires very, very little effort to propel the bowl to a full length jack. Consequently, the bowl sets off at a very slow pace, and takes ages to stop. Indeed, it may take up to 30 seconds on some of those exceptional antipodean greens.

And, the slow green – that is the one with the long grass at the very beginning of our English summer, soft and soggy after a few days' heavy rain – requires a feat of strength to hurl a bowl to a minimum length jack. Consequently, the bowl sets off at a furious pace, but is soon slowed down in its tracks by the long, wet grass,

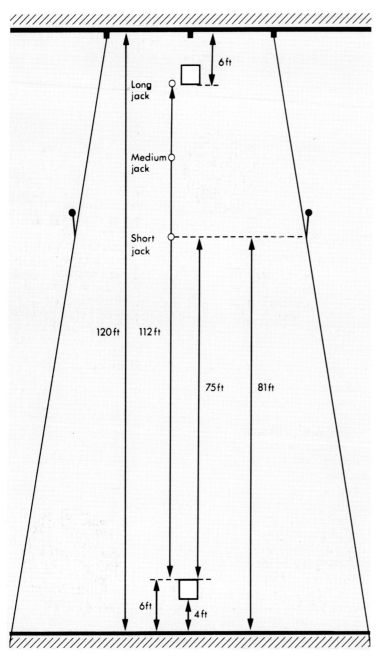

and stops very soon and suddenly. Indeed, it may be travelling for only eight seconds or so on the slowest of British greens.

Indoors, generally, greens are quicker than outdoors, but a lot depends on the quality of the carpet, and, of coure, the underlay. At the height of summer, even in soggy Britain, greens have been known to reach quite fast speeds, significantly faster than most of our indoor carpets, but never in excess of around 18 seconds.

Whatever the speed of the green, it is part of the skill factor of bowls to read the green, estimate the speed, feed the information into the human computer, and adapt to fast and slow surfaces, and short and long jacks. The next question is: how is it done?

Estimating and controlling length

Just as we found with line, there are two distinct processes involved in the mastery of length. The first is theoretical: requiring the ability to recognise, identify and analyse what has to be done. The second is practical: simply doing it!

Both skills can be demonstrated naturally, without any conscious thought about the problem. I tend to encounter, grapple with and solve bowling problems that way – quite naturally. I suppose it is because I was born and bred into bowls, and I never had to go back to basics or think things through in a scientific manner.

That is why writing this book has been such a challenge, forcing me to rationalise some of the actions I have taken for granted for years; yet there are some I still find baffling and, if you excuse me, I am quite content to let them remain so, because of my firm belief that I am a natural, not a studious bowler.

But, to return to the point: first you must be able to read a green, assessing the pace, and the swing (wider, of course, the faster the green); then you must be able to adjust to it.

You must be able to spot the areas of the rink which look as if they will run faster than others, you must be able to tell if your opponent has essayed a subtle change of length (extreme changes are easy to spot and counter!) and you must be able to correct your weight from bowl to bowl.

As far as estimating the length of the jack from the mat is concerned, foreshortening is the bowler's worst enemy, but it is surprising how the human eye, with practice, can allow for such tricks of perspective.

It is worth keeping your eye in by including in your practice routine a session where you are expected to estimate, from the mat end of the green, exactly how far short or through your last delivery was, before your practice partner gives you the information. You will find your guesses illuminating.

As far as adjusting your weight from bowl to bowl is concerned, however intimidated you may feel about being asked by your skip to 'Put another six inches of running on your last bowl,' you must strive to find a way to do it if you can. And although there seems to be no way to guarantee correction of weight other than touch, rhythm and pure natural ability, there are a few practical hints that may help, and they follow on the next pages.

Far Left: The shortest distance permitted between mat and jack is 75 feet, though the IBB has ruled that, for international games, 70 feet will be the minimum distance. On the average green, which is 40 yards long, the longest possible jack at the start of an end is 112 feet, although outdoor greens can be up to 44 yards long.

Left: Viewing from the mat gives a distorted impression. Which of these bowls do you think is short? The bowl beyond the jack appears closer than the bowl short of the jack – until you inspect the position at close quarters (below).

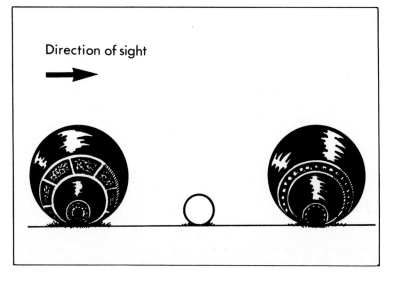

Direction of sight

LENGTH: VARYING BACKSWING AND STEP

If you were going to try to throw a stone a very long distance, you would take your throwing arm a long way back before hurling it.

If you have to try to reach a long jack on a heavy green, the same principles apply –

Right: For fast greens, a short backswing helps to reduce impulsion.

Below: For average greens, a medium backswing should be employed.
Below Right: For heavy greens, a long backswing is necessary.

and the same solution may be found. A long backswing is helpful when the green is slow, and, it follows that a short backswing makes bowling simpler on fast greens where it is difficult 'to hold them back'.

The experienced New Zealander, Phil Skoglund, whom I beat in the final of the Embassy world indoor singles at Coatbridge in 1986, plays at Palmerston North, where the greens are exceptionally fast, and his delivery has the most exaggerated backswing I have ever seen!

It just does not make sense – until you realise that, although his backswing takes the bowl as high as his head, Phil's forward swing suddenly decelerates as it nears the point of release, and, effectively, he bowls off a very short swing indeed.

I do not consciously lengthen or shorten my backswing to cope with extreme conditions of pace, but I am sure that I must do it naturally – another example, perhaps, of what one player does naturally proving a useful coaching example for another player who may be looking for some help with a particular problem.

LENGTH: OF THE STEP

If you were going to try to throw a javelin a very long distance, you would take some extra long strides as part of your run-up.

If you have to try to reach a long jack on a heavy green, the same principles apply – and the same solution may be found. A long forward step is helpful when the green is slow, and it follows that a shorter forward step – or no step at all – is better on fast greens.

When I played in Australia in the Mazda series for the Aussie Jack High title, I found myself taking a very short step, and keeping my back foot (the right one) anchored on the mat, rather like a crown green bowler – but for a different reason. It is a crown code rule that one foot should be kept on the mat, but I was doing it simply to cut down on my natural forward movement.

Again, this was something that I did without thinking about it – a natural reflex, almost, to the conditions which were at that time beyond my previous experience. I found it worked a treat. Why don't you try it next time you come across a very fast green?

Remember, take a short step on a fast green, a medium step on a medium-paced green and a long step on a heavy green. Some bowlers even deliberately take a short step when playing to a short jack, a medium step when playing to a medium-length jack and a long step when playing to a long jack.

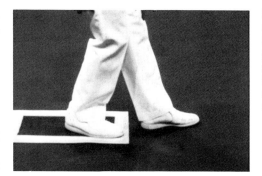

On fast greens, use a short step forward (top). On average greens, use a medium step forward (centre). On heavy greens, use a long step forward (bottom).

❛Take a normal step in New Zealand and your bowl will not stop on the green. When you play for a while on very fast greens, you adapt your forward step so that it is much shorter than it would be in Britain, on slow to medium-paced greens. There is such a great need to modify one's delivery when one visits New Zealand or Australia that the governing bodies really should make sure that enough time is given for our national teams to acclimatise when we contest the Commonwealth Games or World Bowls in the southern hemisphere.❜

LENGTH: SPEED OF FORWARD SWING AND THRUST

If you were going to try to throw a cricket ball from the boundary to the wicket, you would move your throwing arm at some considerable speed – in fact as fast as you could.

If you are trying to reach a long jack on a heavy green, the same principles apply – and the same solution may be found. A speeded up forward swing is helpful when the green is slow, and it follows that a slowed down arm action can work well on fast greens.

Slow motion movement demands a great deal of control, however, and it can be seen why playing on very fast greens is a real test of finesse.

This way of achieving control of length is the method I employ, but it wasn't until recently that I realised it. Watching a video recording of one of my televised matches, it occurred to me that I have always given the momentum of the bowl a boost during the final stages of my forward swing.

Above: On heavy greens, you will have to speed up your action, especially your forward swing.

Right: On average greens, use an easy, natural, medium-paced forward swing.

Far Right: On fast greens, slow down your action, especially your forward swing.

Thrust of fingers, hand and wrist

If you were going to try to throw a stone a little bit further than you did the first time, you would give it an extra flick with your fingers, and even use your wrist to get a bit more 'torque'.

If you fall short with your first bowl, the same principles apply – and you can attempt to adjust with your next by using your fingers or your wrist as last moment boosters. My delivery is a classic example.

Even in my basic delivery, I make much of the power-assisted forearm movement which augments the otherwise fairly orthodox pendulum swing. The control I have over length – such as it is – I feel with my fingers, as it is these that impel the bowl, and add a fine tuning element to the momentum generated by the swing itself.

I think it must be made clear that big adjustments will be made using the length and speed of the swing and the size of the step, and the adjustments made by the fingers, hand and wrist will be minor. Any attempt to use these for bigger scale correction would result in the bowl being thrown, chucked or hurled down the green, and I don't think we should resort to that, even on the heaviest brute of a green.

The other thing that should be stressed here is that even the fine movements should be carefully aligned with all the 'straight line' placements and movements outlined on previous pages, or all your good work on finding the right line will be wasted.

Using your wrist, hand and fingers can give some power-assistance, helping to push the bowl a bit further on heavy greens – and even giving some fine control on fast greens.

LENGTH: USE OF BODY WEIGHT AND MOVEMENT

‘ Coming off our indoor greens in the spring onto 'woolly' outdoor greens can be a bit of a shock. This is the time to let your hair down and play uninhibited bowls, putting your body weight behind your bowl with gusto. Don't be neat and careful. Don't even try to find a delicate touch. Get those bowls up the green any way you can. But try to keep a good line all the time. 🔳

Scottish runners put body weight into their delivery to reach the jack on heavy greens.

If you were going to try to throw a javelin even further than last time, you would enthusiastically put all your body into the effort of chucking it out of sight.

The same principle applies in bowls, and it is especially necessary on some of our outdoor greens early in the season to use your body weight and your shoulder as you attempt to reach a long jack.

The snag is that, in your effort to summon up all your strength, you run the risk of sacrificing your accuracy. You see the same thing happen when people try to fire too fast when they should be using what we call 'controlled weight' (see pages 68 to 79). Fast bowlers of another kind – in cricket – suffer from the same problem when they try to bowl *too* fast.

Of course, the reason for a loss of accuracy is simply that in going for speed, there is too little attention paid to line, and some of the extra movements which have been introduced to add a few extra miles per hour have been allowed rather sloppily to be made out of or across the line.

Whether you are firing or just 'being up', there will be no problem if you can find a way of being faithful to the line. And if that

seems to repeat words that have already been used on previous pages that only serves to underline just how important 'straight line' movements can be.

Putting your body weight into your drawing shot is vital in the United Kingdom, but it is unheard of in Australia and New Zealand, where any clumsily applied extra weight going into your delivery guarantees the bowl's unimpeded progress into the ditch at the far end.

Body weight, imparted by on-line body movement, then, is invaluable for coping with heavy greens and making big scale, family-sized adjustment of length, but is best left alone when minor corrections are called for.

ALLCOCK'S TIP

● *On a heavy green, if you are not careful, the tendency is to keep your actions small, and heave the bowl. This can induce faults in your line. Exaggerate your movements, swing your arm freely, and you will find it a lot easier. Loosen up.*

LENGTH: BOWLING THE JACK

Every top bowler regards the bowling of the jack as a vital skill. Mistakes with the jack have been known to lose matches, so just as much concentration must go into your jack-throwing (although, I must say I don't like that term) as you devote to delivering your woods.

Again, there are two skills involved: the first comes under the heading of tactical theory; the second is all about practical technique. First you have to decide where to deliver the jack to give yourself and your team an advantage, then you have to be able physically to produce the goods and put the jack where you want it.

Most top bowlers have no real preference when it comes to length of jack. They reckon they can bowl them all. But, as you have no doubt noticed, every game of bowls takes on a shape and character of its own. One player will struggle at a certain length at which his opponent excels, and jack tactics become a major feature.

Sometimes that is because the player with the wide-bias bowls is unable to cope with the extra green he has to take on long jacks; or perhaps the player with the straighter woods is forever finding the 'runs' in the green on the shorter jacks.

In such a case, not only must you be able to recognise your opponent's weakness, but you must be able to exploit it through skilful control of the jack.

If jack control is such a vital factor, it is surprising that we don't see bowlers out there on the green practising their casting of the jack. I recommend taking eight jacks (if they are available) out on your rink, and putting in as much serious practice with them as you would with your woods.

Practising line with the jack

Indeed, there may well be profitable spin-off. The jack, in flat green bowls at any rate, has no bias, so there is an immediate measure available to assess your success as a 'straight line' deliverer. Not that it matters whether you bowl the jack in a straight line or not, because it will always, in a match, be centred by your skip or the marker, but, while you are practising, you might as well make use of your time by

honing your line as well as your length.

Incidentally, there are ploys that can be used to make jack control easier. If you have brought the mat well up the green, it can be quite an intimidating challenge to keep the jack on the green. After all, you must steer it to within two yards (0.6m) of the ditch. Not much margin for error.

Check the green at that far end. If there is an area where the grass is longer quite near the ditch (there quite often is!) it will pay you to take advantage of it and roll the jack towards that lusher region, so that, if you accidentally overbowl, the grass will save you and stop the jack actually reaching the ditch.

Above: Mistakes with the jack can lose matches. Practise the art – and give it as much concentration as you devote to your woods.

THE DRAW: TO AN OPEN JACK

When I won the Embassy World indoor title in 1986, I reckon it was my first two bowls that did it for me. And Hugh Duff, the brilliant young Scotsman, certainly showed everyone how to draw when he won the title in 1988. In singles, it really is the first two bowls that set the pattern, and establish the initiative. The same thing applies to team games. That's how important the lead is in a four.

The draw is both the basic and the simplest shot in the game. All you have to do it put those two commodities, line and length together, and your bowl will finish on the required spot on the green. That is the perfect draw, and anything more pleasurable and satisfying than seeing your bowl nestle up to the jack after having finished its curving course down the rink is difficult to imagine.

Drawing is the term used by bowlers to denote that only enough weight is being used in their shot to take their bowl as far as the object – normally, but not always, the jack. Exact control of weight is called for, as the attempt to draw will have been said to have failed if you finish a yard (1m) short of your target, or a similar distance through. Even a foot (30cm) away from the target is often not good enough.

Over the next few pages we will look at the different types of draw that you may be expected to perform, but it may be useful to remember that, in a way, they are all the same. If you take the right line and the right length, you will achieve them all!

Indeed, even the weighted shots described later can be looked upon as drawing shots, as they are also delivered on a given line and at a given weight, and if there were no obstacle – like the head you may be trying to hit – in the way, your bowl would, given a big enough green, stop eventually when it ran out of steam! Its course, in that case, would be called the draw. If you look at it that way, there is no real difference between a drive (see pages 76 to 79) and a draw.

The basic shot

If drawing is basic to bowls, then drawing to an open jack in its rightful place, on the centre line of the rink, and with no previous woods littering your path to success, must be the most basic shot of all. Surprising, then, that most experts agree that, to execute that shot in a team game you need a specialist player who is called a lead.

It seems to me that, if you aspire to call yourself a bowler, you should strive for mastery of that most basic shot of all. And, although I have the highest regard for the superb specialist leads I have been privileged to know, I would say, without any disrespect to them, that, if I felt I couldn't play lead and hold my own with the best of them, I think I should give up the game.

Why then, the need for a specialist? Simple the shot may be, but there are pressures on the lead that I will try to analyse on page 83. Leading is a single-minded occupation needing patience and a good temperament, but at least you have all your time available for concentrating on the two main factors – line and length – for you never have to play a weighted wood.

Forehand and backhand leads

The first thing to do is to choose the side of the rink you think is the truest – and therefore the most likely to enable you to get your wood near the jack. Unless you have cause to change your mind later in the match, stick to the same side of the rink throughout. That means playing forehand one way and backhand the other, so it is clear, even at lead, that there is no place for a bowler who can only play one hand.

Occasionally you may come across a rink where the best hands available are the opposite sides of the rink – say, forehand one way, and forehand the other as well. You must be quick to recognise this, and to decide to go along with the unorthodox practice of 'playing round the clock' as it is called. Ideally it is better to stick to the one side of the rink because often pace varies from one side to the other.

Drawing to an open jack: there's nothing quite like it. There is nothing already up there to help or hinder you – you're on your own. Whether you are a lead or a skip, it's a shot you should practise and practise.

ALLCOCK'S TIP

● *I would always bank on a drawing bowler to beat a driving bowler – on the law of averages. Practise the more glamorous shots by all means, but do not neglect the basic shot in the game. It really is what bowls is all about.*

Drawing: bowl along the right line and give it the right weight — your bowl will finish on the jack every time.

THE DRAW: TO A DISPLACED JACK

' In my new role as commentator with ITV, I have been forced to become a good spectator. One of the things I have noticed, indoors, is how bowlers playing to a displaced jack tend to put on a bit more weight than is necessary, and go through too far. What they are doing is allowing for the heavier bit of green out near the string, having got into the habit outdoors. But the same thing just does not apply indoors, and they are invariably caught out. Felt does not respond to constant rolling by becoming quicker in the way that grass does. '

Whereas the specialist lead has to concentrate on drawing to the jack in its original position in the centre of the rink, back-end players often have to draw to a jack which has been displaced – sometimes dramatically – by an accurate heavy delivery. Although the new shot called for seems to make the same demands as those faced by the lead, there are several possible variables which need to be considered carefully.

The first is a matter of line. If the green were perfectly uniform, it would be easy, but greens rarely are, I'm afraid. So, flat green bowlers must become speculators, rather like their crown green counterparts who can't possibly know exactly where the correct line to the jack can be when they are continually using a new bit of ground.

On an outdoor green, especially a soft one like those we have in Britain, the new line is likely to be *straighter* than the normal road to the jack. The fresh grass you will be traversing will not have been rolled flat like the grass where most of the play has taken place. Use your powers of observation, and check for yourself whether the grass on the road you intend using appears longer or greener than elsewhere. If it does, be prepared for the line to be tighter than you might expect.

The second consideration, arising from the very same factors, is length. Of course, if your bowl is rolling over comparatively long grass on hitherto unused territory, you can expect to have to use *more weight* than if you were bowling to a similar length jack on the centre line.

When you are practising, don't invariably straighten the jack before you bowl – although that is what I see most people doing. Why not leave it where it stops? Bowling to a non-centred jack will make you much more adaptable, and much more conscious of watching every delivery like a hawk, because you will never become complacent about your line – that really is something I have learnt from my crown green friends.

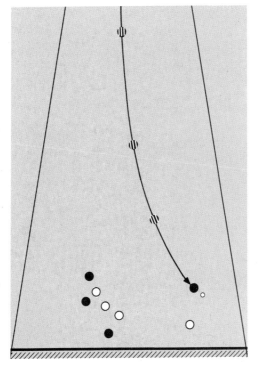

When bowling to a displaced jack, you must look for a new line – use your powers of observation.

THE DRAW: TO THE BRINK OF A DITCH

One of the most spectacular shots in bowls is the draw to the brink of the ditch when the jack has been buried and hidden from view. The ability to retrieve from such a situation shows skill and nerve, for, although the shot is still a basic draw to a given spot, the penalty for being just an inch or so heavy is losing your bowl, losing the shot, and, possibly, losing the match.

Chances are that, adding to the pressure of the situation is the nagging knowledge that as well as finding a new length, the jack is, in all probability, off-centre, and a new line will have to be found.

Sometimes it pays not to be too adventurous with your first bowl – assuming you have two left after your opponent's brilliant ditcher. Look carefully at the position. If you are just one down, and you've got only inches to draw the shot, you might as well go for gold and try to bowl the perfect shot. If you are bit too heavy, you're still only one down!

But, if you are several shots down, some of them are likely to be quite some way from the jack, still in the position they occupied before the head was disturbed and the jack trailed. Then the shot you must play is entirely different. Rather than arrogantly going for the sensational, and trying to draw the number one shot, your first priority will be to get second wood, or at least a saving bowl, before trying to impress everyone with your phenomenal accuracy with your next bowl.

I do not often see bowlers practising the draw shot to the edge of the rink. I am sure it would help them when it came to facing unnerving situations in a competitive match if more attention were to be paid to such broken play set-ups in practice.

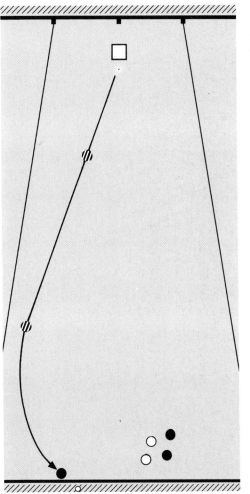

How much margin for error have you got? What are your realistic chances of getting the shot? Is it vital to get the shot? Is it easier/safer to make sure of getting second? What are the consequences of failure? These are the sorts of questions you should be asking yourself as you face a draw to the brink of the ditch.

If you are the skip, discuss it with your your third – and with the rest of your rink – and, when you have decided where you want your bowl to finish, get your third to stand in position to give you some visual assistance. You will not want to be heavy – that much is obvious! But you won't want to finish in an exposed position either. It's a difficult decision to make – and a difficult shot to play.

A test of nerve – just an inch or so heavy and you lose your bowl.

THE DRAW: FOR SECOND WOOD OR POSITION

' When you decide that discretion is the better part of valour and go for second rather than playing the spectacular shot, it is surprising how often you get a bonus by drawing the number one shot which previously appeared impossible. **'**

Drawing, in a way, is often regarded as a safe, conservative shot, lacking in gusto, drama, and imagination. Believe me, a good drawing shot, under pressure, may be less drastic a solution to a crisis, but there is no sense in which it is a soft option. A saving draw, whether it takes the shot or not, can be, in my opinion, the most exciting shot in bowls.

Getting the shot is not everything. All the time, you must consider the priorities – just as we did when the jack was in the ditch, on page 57. It may look possible to make a few shots with a risky attempt at a trail; it may look easy to get the shot by using weight: but, if you are several shots down in the head, your priority must be to save, and a draw for second wood may the best way of doing that.

Indeed, drawing successfully for second shot may be enough to win you the game when you come to look back on it afterwards. It may be conservative, but there is nothing chicken or yellow-bellied about it at all. Such tight, defensive bowling can have a demoralising effect on the opposition, if every time they appear to be heading for a count, the chance is stolen from them by a 'simple' draw.

Treat the shot exactly as you would a straightforward draw to the jack. Don't be affected by the consequences of failure. Such reaction to pressure may be understandable, but it is counter-productive. I realise that it is easier said than done, but it is essential to play the pressure shots as calmly as you would the easy ones.

Again, I would recommend the advantages of practising the draw for second shot. Borrow some bowls and compose a typical head with several shots against, but an open draw for second, and see how many times you can achieve your objective. It may raise a few eyebrows in the clubhouse, but, if you're a serious student of the game, you won't care a fig about that!

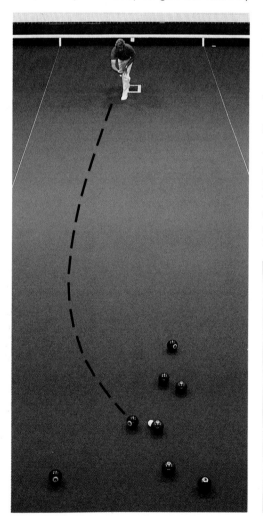

Right: Drawing a good second is one of the most valuable shots in the game.

ALLCOCK'S TIP

● *Playing defensively I confess is not really in my nature, but it is something I have learnt as I have matured. Being patient when you are in trouble and trying to minimise the damage can pay dividends later on, when you win a match you should really have been out of by the half-way stage.*

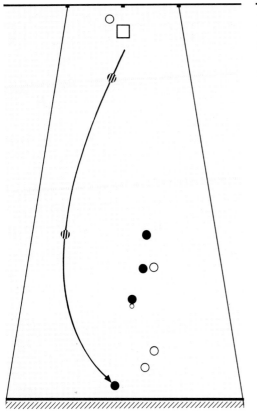

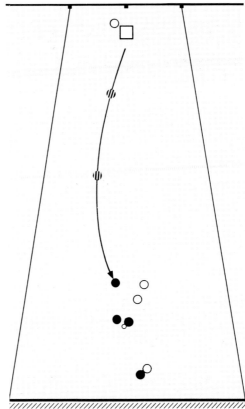

The draw for position

When you hold the shot, and you want to keep it, it sometimes pays to keep well away from the head. Then is the time to decide whether you need a short bowl to guard your shot, or a back bowl to receive the jack if it is struck by your opponent. This is called 'drawing for position'.

The one thing that should make the positional draw easier is the very thing that, in a way, makes it more difficult. By the nature of the shot, it is employed normally when the player is sitting pretty – and therein lies the danger. If care is not taken, the shot will be played casually, as if it is not very important for it to succeed.

Believe me, it is. Positional shots are every bit as important as the more spectacular shot-getting and shot-saving efforts that are more likely to be remembered. So, take real care in assessing the need for a positional wood rather than another shot, in identifying exactly where you need your positional wood, and, most of all, in your attempt to draw a bowl into that position. It could win you the game.

The easiest position to find is normally the insurance bowl round the back. Assuming that your route is not blocked, it should be a formality to achieve it. And,

often, the location does not have to be precise. Perhaps all you need is the 'best back', to ensure that, if the jack flies into the ditch, you will score the shot – or at worst drop only one.

The short blocker

The hardest position to find is always the short bowl, known as the block, blocker, guard or policeman. This deterrent bowl, intended to stop the opponent's access to the head, is notoriously difficult because it has to be positioned in exactly the right place if his line is to be effectively stopped.

A few inches out, and the shot he wanted is still available. Indeed, even if you get everything right, and your blocker finishes perfectly, a skilful opponent may still be able to find a way inside it with more weight than he had intended, or outside it with less.

On occasions, the best position for your final delivery is going to be neither in front nor behind. Sometimes, when, for example, the jack is touching a bowl, the likely path of a disturbed jack will be easy to predict. Then you will want to position a bowl, maybe jack high (level with the jack) or even on the string (the side boundary of the rink).

> Top players who consider positional play to be a waste of time do not deserve the name. Look carefully at the head. Consider the options open to the opposition – not only the likely ones, but the unlikely ones as well. Your opponent might be unorthodox, desperate, or just plain lucky. What result could he possibly get that would lbe disastrous from your point of view? Cover it. If you don't, you may be made to regret it.

Above Left: The back bowl is relatively easy to play – but try to place it accurately, for best effect.

Above Right: The blocker is difficult to place accurately, but it can be a killer.

THE YARD-ON SHOT

The yard-on shot can produce dramatic head-turning and match-winning results.

So far we have referred only to the drawing shot, which, although it may be the basic and most important of all, is not the only shot in the book. A complete player will have a full repertoire of shots at his disposal, and, even if he doesn't always have to use them all, will be more successful and confident as a bowler because he is versatile.

The yard-on shot is a natural extension of the draw shot. Games have been swung by a delicate movement of the jack to make a big score out of nothing. That sort of shot is called a 'trail', and is little more than a 'reaching draw', which is another term by which it is frequently known.

When your skip asks you to 'be up to the head', he probably wants you to play a heavy draw, 'making sure you reach'. He doesn't want you to fire, merely to ensure you use more than the exact weight you would be using if you were drawing, and to bowl 'through the head'.

The shot must be played with fractionally more weight than you need for the draw, and, of course, with fractionally less green as well, or you will be disappointed to see your bowl sail by the head and finish

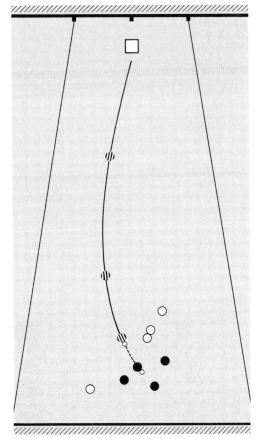

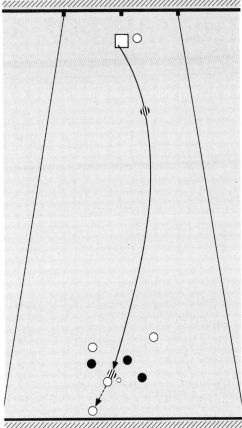

Trailing for a count is something of a lottery. Don't attempt it unless you are really well placed. Only play it if it doesn't really matter if you fail. It's a bonus shot.

When attempting a trail, think of it as a draw to a position a little way behind and a bit narrow of the jack. If you pick up the jack en route, so much the better.

Far Left: A good trail can give you a 'bucketful' of shots.

Left: Easing an enemy bowl out of the head. A bowl is bigger than the jack, and a more inviting target.

a yard behind on the centre line – not a bad position, but not what your skip asked for at all.

This is definitely a shot to be practised regularly, as it is significantly (if only subtly) different from the pure draw, and is not an easy shot, especially for the beginner, who is striving manfully to get to terms with the basic drawing shot without any frills.

Trailing for a count

If you have built up a good position, with a cluster of bowls just behind the jack, the head is said to be in your favour, for, even if there are shots against you, you can nullify your opponent's shots advantage by trailing the jack gently for a big count.

Just a word of warning: don't be fooled into spending all your efforts playing weight and trying to move the jack if there is a danger of your opponent piling more and more shots into the head and scoring a bundle himself.

You can just as well play the trail for a 'bucketful' after you have played the more defensive 'draw to save' as outlined on page 58. So be patient, and learn to play the more spectacular and profitable shot

when the time is right.

What a morale-booster it is, though, when you achieve that turn-over trail by moving the jack perhaps less than a foot (30cm) or so, but depriving your opponent of shots he has worked hard to establish. With luck, it will hit him as hard, and it will certainly lift your team.

Just remember the technique: a touch more weight and a shade less green.

The gentle take-out

A similar shot, played with the same weight, is the gentle take-out, when, with very little more than drawing strength, you ease an enemy bowl out of the head for a count. In a way, this is an easier shot than the trail, a bowl being about twice as wide as a jack, and therefore an easier target.

First look at the dangers – you might snick the jack accidentally in passing – before playing the shot as a natural draw, with confidence. The temptation is always to use too much weight, so don't get too excited. Play it calmly, with control, with a touch more weight and a fraction less green than if you were drawing to the target bowl.

THE YARD-ON SHOT: REMOVING A DANGER OR TUCKING THE JACK

Tucking the jack around the corner and out of sight is always a good idea.

Sometimes, even when you may hold the shot, there may be such considerable danger of a trail by the opposition that you may decide to attempt to trail the jack away from your own shot bowl, to take away the danger.

Perhaps the head has developed so that you have back bowls on one side of the head, while your opponent has the better back position on the other. That may be the time to take a risk, accepting the danger of giving the shot away, but depriving your opponent of a chance he would have relished.

On an occasion like this, a bird in the hand is worth very little, for it is your adversary who will be looking for the two in the bush!

This, of course, is the sort of shot to play

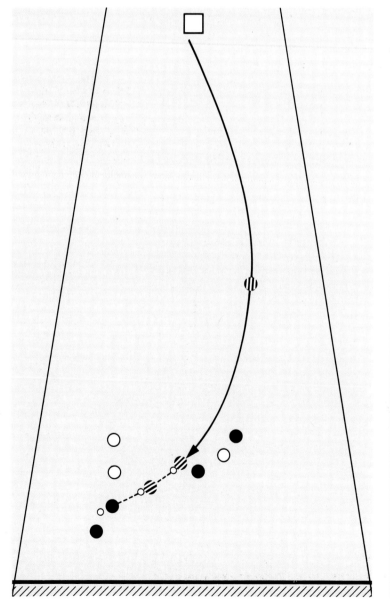

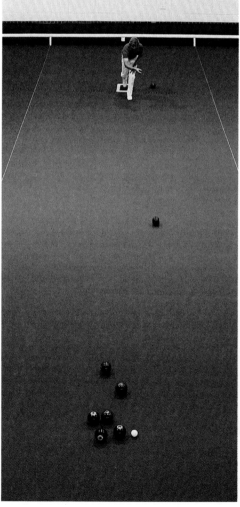

when you still have at least one bowl left to play, for your must face the fact that there is an element of danger in the shot, and it might go against you. If you are the skip, it is the sort of shot you might ask your number three to play!

Tucking the Jack

One of the worst positions for your shot wood to lie is alongside the jack – jack high – where it can be seen from the mat, and where it offers an inviting target to the man who likes to 'be up'.

In such a position it is as well to be bold and 'be up' yourself, for, if you trail the jack 'around the corner' you may hold a better shot. Indeed, your wood which was shot may now be in a position which affords some protection – in other words, in the way!

Tighten your line, increase your weight almost imperceptibly, merely making sure you are going to reach and maybe giving the bowl a little more of a send-off with the tips of the fingers. Touch the jack in passing and you tuck it round the corner, putting it out of sight and much more difficult to get at. Pick it up clean and you again, with a bit of luck, put it out of sight.

Resting (pushing and replacing) your own shot bowl gives you a good wood behind the jack, and the chance that the new shot will be in a slightly more difficult position for your opponent. Even if you miss your target altogether, you achieve a great positional bowl, up to a yard behind the jack which your opposite number is likely to be attacking.

The moral to the tale is: 'Be positive'. Don't be negative when you are holding shot, especially when it is easily beaten by the opposition. Don't be afraid of re-arranging the head; it is frustrating for your opponent to be faced with a different problem every time he steps on to the mat to bowl a wood.

‘I believe in attacking the head even when it is in my favour. If *I* don't attack it, my opponent probably will, so I might as well get in before him. Of course, when I talk of attacking the head, I don't mean giving it a real thump – merely the idea of reaching the jack with a yard or less. Playing positive. ,

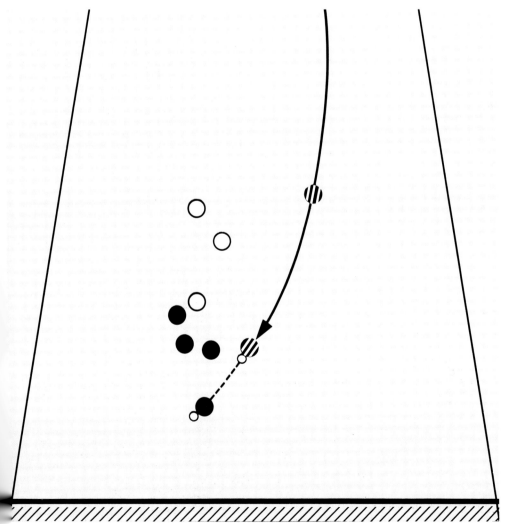

Left: Sometimes it pays to be bold – it may be worth taking a risk, even if you are already holding the shot.

THE YARD-ON SHOT: PROMOTING A BOWL OR CHANGING THE HEAD

‟ To promote your own bowl presupposes you have a short bowl in a useful position, so this shot can be regarded as consolidation of a good position rather than a way of making something out of nothing. ”

Cut your green, increase your weight fractionally, and your short bowls can sometimes be of use to you.

Promotion is what happens when you push your own, slightly short bowl into the count. What you call it when you push your opponent's bowl into the count is unprintable, but involves very much the same technique.

Again you cut your green, narrowing the angle of your delivery by a fraction. Again you urge the bowl on its course with a little more weight than is required for a dead length draw. Some skips ask their men to 'press' into the head – and I feel that term speaks for itself.

If it helps – and this applies to all the weighted shots described here – you can

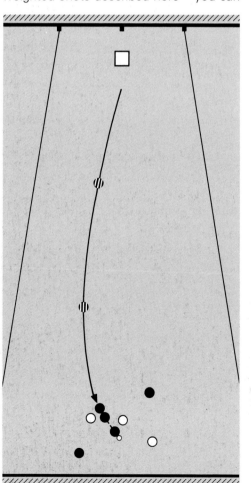

regard the yard-on shot as a draw, but a draw, not to the jack of course, but to a position behind the head. Identify the position you would be drawing to for the bowl to pass 'through' the head at the weight required to have the desired effect.

In the case of promotion, the weight needed to turn a bowl over once or twice will vary considerably according to the pace of the green you are playing on. On a reasonably fast surface, a true yard-on shot will be sufficient to do the deed. On a heavy green the wood you want to promote may need a hefty wallop before it can be persuaded to turn over. Then you will be looking for something rather more generous than an honest yard-on shot – but the basic principles will be the same.

You really need to get out there and work it out in practice. Reading about it is a poor substitute for the real thing.

ALLCOCK'S TIP

● *With all these yard-on shots, it is important to test the green at an early stage to see if it is the kind of surface which will allow the shot to be played at all. Sometimes you can get a hand which reacts badly to a yard-on shot. Every time you cut the green and put on a little weight, you will find the bowl refuses to arc, and 'hangs off', passing the target on the outside.*

Typically, this kind of hand continues to show the same quality even when you give first a little less green, then less still, then even less – until you reach a kind of watershed, where suddenly, 'whoosh', your bowl whips away wildly, out of all proportion to the green you have given it, and finishes well tight. If you are up against a hand like that, leave the yard-on shot well alone.

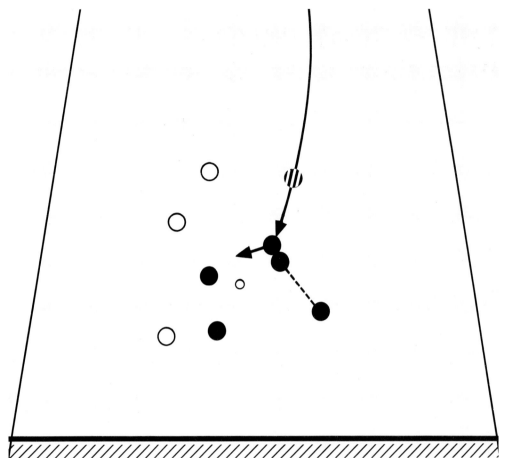

Changing the shape of the head

I have mentioned before (on page 63) that there are advantages in attacking a favour-able head – within reason. If you hold shots, your opponent's thinking will be occupied in planning his offensive. If by the time he gets to the mat the head has changed, he will have to rethink his battle plan, and you will have retained the initiative.

A reaching draw is an effective weapon in this respect: not heavy enough – just one yard of weight, remember – to do any damage, but with enough running to shuffle things around a bit. Of course you will not be trying anything so adventurous when things in the head are at all precari-ous, or indeed if your shot bowl is extreme-ly safe where it is.

Then you would be thinking positionally (see page 59). But, if the head is evenly balanced and accessible to your opponent, you might as well be bold and try to add another shot and rearrange the head. With luck, the rearrangement could prove to be in your favour. If not, you can always try again.

If the head looks inviting to your opponent, it's worth shuffling things around a bit, hoping to improve the lie.

THE YARD-ON SHOT: THE WICK AND THE PLANT

❝ I remember how Willie Paul, a very consistent Scottish lead, was devastated in the final of the British Isles singles championship at Worthing in 1986, when Wynne Richards was blessed with an outrageous wick off a bowl at least four yards short, came in for shot, and went on to win a game he should have lost. That's the sort of luck you just have to shrug off if it happens against you, but a played-for wick deserves applause. ❞

All top bowlers talk about the 'percentage shot'. They refer to a bowl delivered with a specific aim in mind, but with secondary targets if their prime objective fails.

Such secondary targets are often known as wicks, glides, ricochets or feathers in polite circles, while less polite, uninitiated bowlers have been known to inspect ironically the soles of the perpetrators' bowling shoes to discover what, if anything, they stepped in on the way to the bowling club!

Many regard David Bryant as a lucky bowler. If he appears to be it is because he is the master of the percentage shot. If he misses his number one aim, there are often several second choices available to him.

A wick is a contact with another bowl which changes the course of your delivery – exactly like a cannon in snooker. A glide is less extreme, and the change of direction less pronounced. A ricochet is another

word for wick, while a feather is the merest touch on the jack or a bowl, which causes virtually no change of direction at all, but possibly reduces the running on the bowl to the advantage or disadvantage of the bowler.

The one thing that all percentage bowls must have in common is weight. They must carry enough extra running to give them that second chance if the first choice goes begging. Wicks take weight off a bowl, so if a wick or a glide is going to carry a slightly wayward wood on to the jack, it must have had more than exact drawing weight in the first place.

Not all wicks and glides are second choices. Sometimes the head is so blocked up that there is no chance of getting the shot without using weight and going for a ricochet. Not a lot of weight may be required and the yard-on shot is ideal for the purpose.

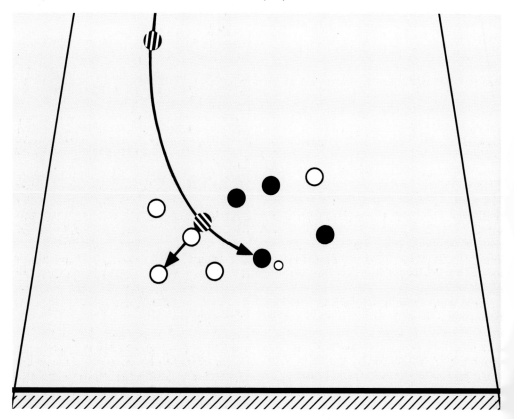

Sometimes playing for a 'wick' is the best way of getting the shot.

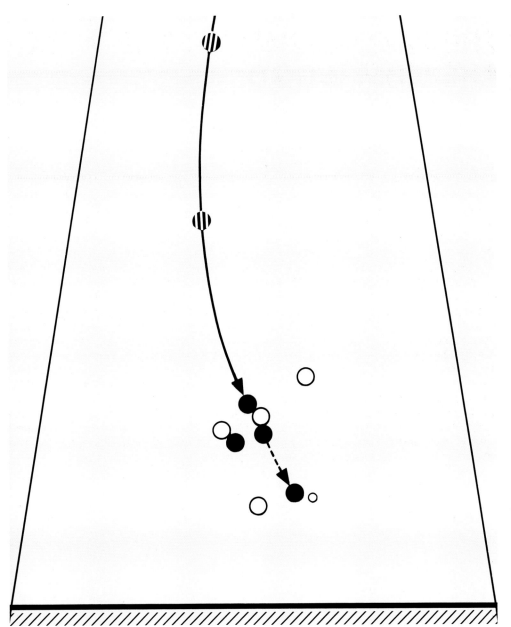

❛Beware the temptation to play a gentle plant with too much weight. Often the yard-on shot is the best one to play. More weight would often be too destructive, and, as every bowler knows, accidents do happen. The more weight you use, the more liable you are to accidents, as a general rule. ❜

When two bowls are touching, it is possible to predict exactly where one bowl will go when the other one is struck. Such playing of a plant is often a good way of getting the shot.

The gentle plant

The plant, as in snooker, is often seen as a useful way of getting the shot, especially when the drawing approaches to the jack have been blocked up. Top bowlers think like snooker players, and are always on the look-out for plants, cannons, wicks and glides.

Preferably the plant consists of two bowls that are actually touching each other. Then it is possible to predict with accuracy exactly where one bowl will go when the other one is struck.

When trying to promote your own bowl by means of a plant, not much weight will be required to turn the bowl into the head.

The dynamic tension between the two touching bowls is sufficient to ensure that a sharp tap on the one will send the other some way – although, naturally, it will travel further on a fast green than a slow one. A yard of weight will probably be quite enough, so the yard-on shot will again be ideal for the purpose. Practise the shot thoroughly until the control of weight becomes natural.

And try to remember that a yard of weight really means a yard of weight – not five or ten or fifteen. Be precise in your use of the term, both when playing the shot yourself, and when, as a skip, you give instructions to your team.

THE TIMING-SHOT: THE FIRM WOOD

The timing-shot is an important part of my game. It can be an exciting shot to play and can do a lot of damage.

Drawing and firing – at the two ends of the weight spectrum – must be well known features of bowls, even, through television, to non-playing members of the general public. The more subtle variations of weight between these two extremes are less well known, and, I would say, not all that well understood by bowlers at large.

The right weight for the right shot: that should be the aim of every bowler. Not only the understanding of angles and impact, so that the appropriate weight can be intelligently chosen, but the versatility to play the full range of weights with complete control.

One of the most useful weighted shots in my repertoire is the timing-shot, and I confess that it is a real favourite of mine when I am forced to get myself out of trouble, and when an all-out firing shot is neither necessary nor desirable. There are occasions, too, when the drive is simply out of the question, and the timing shot really comes into its own.

What is the timing-shot? The phrase itself I picked up in Scotland, and I liked the way it conveyed the kind of shot it refers to. The bowl is delivered firmly, not fired, under perfect control, with an action very similar if not identical with that used for a draw. There is enough weight behind it for it to reach the ditch if it is unobstructed, but not so much that it runs straight.

The timing-shot, as its name suggests, allows time for the bowl to bend with the bias, and as a result, is not the easiest shot to judge. I find I can be quite accurate with it, and have had a fair amount of success when I have been reduced to using it. For, make no mistake, the primary function of the timing shot is to destroy.

As we shall see, there are positive reasons for using the timing-shot, and often it is to be preferred to the drive. Like the other shots described in this book it needs practice before it can enter the repertoire of the complete bowler.

1-4 The positive, aggressive take-out can yield many a good count.

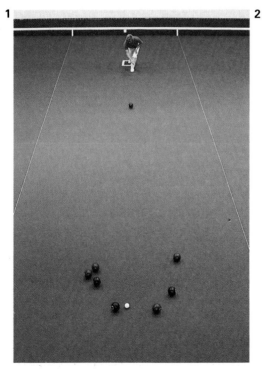

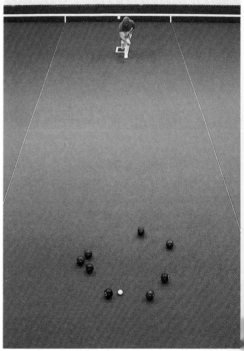

THE TIMING-SHOT: THE TAKE OUT

As we saw on page 61, the yard-on shot can be used to take out your opponent's nearest bowl and claim a count for yourself. There are times, however, when you might want to push the enemy bowl more than a couple of turns out of the head, or when the neat near-drawing line is, for some reason, not available.

Then is the time to resort to something more positive, like the aggressive timing-shot. Because of the control that is part and parcel of the shot, it can be used with confidence to strike a single bowl target, without undue worries of being off-target.

ALLCOCK'S TIP

● *Before you can take chances with timing-shots, you have to have got to be confident of drawing yourself out of trouble with your next bowl if you miss. That is why it is not really a shot for the novice.*

One word of warning: when deciding which hand to play the shot on, give careful consideration to the dangers of the shot and to the qualities of the two sides of the rink – one side might well swing more than the other, and this propensity to swing with weight may bear little relationship to the normal swing of the draw on each hand.

The best thing to do is to watch like a hawk when your opponents play weight, and learn, if you can, from their mistakes! It's a shame, in a way, that bowlers are not normally allowed more than two trial ends before embarking on a match, even at high level competition, so there is not time to experiment with a variety of weighted shots, and the priority must be to master the draw on the trial ends.

Another word of advice: use the swinging-with-weight feature to effect your take-outs across the head, so the swing of the bowl is forever taking it away from the head and out of trouble rather than towards it and potential disaster.

❛The timing-shot is one of my favourite shots. Think of it as a semi-drive, and use it in preference to the all-out firing shot, especially on heavy greens. Peter Belliss, a famous firer, soon found out, on his first visit to Worthing, that firing is a hazardous business on our soggy British greens. Now he uses controlled weight when he plays in the United Kingdom. Rethinking his own game (the typical draw/drive Kiwi approach) Peter adapted with such success that he won the World outdoor singles at Aberdeen in 1984. The timing shot is now very much part of Belliss's armoury.❜

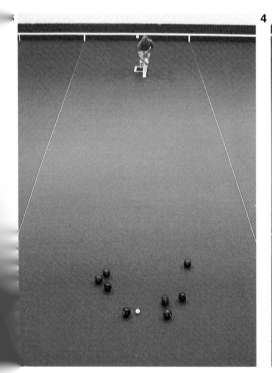
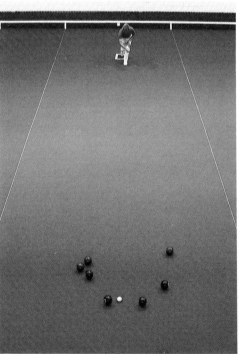

THE TIMING-SHOT: DITCHING THE JACK, WICKS AND SPLITS

In Australia and New Zealand, they are prepared to risk wasting an early delivery on a firing attempt. If the opponent gets close with his first, they are adventurous enough to have a go at it, even with their first bowl. After all, they have another three bowls to come with which to fight a rearguard action.

I tend to think the same way. It has earned me the reputation of being unorthodox, but I am prepared, on occasions, to take chances with, say, my second delivery, as, when you are playing well and with confidence, an early killer can deal a big psychological blow.

Right: If you can ditch the jack as I did in the end illustrated, you will sap your opponent's confidence.

Far Right: A yard of weight to obtain a wick.

When an adverse position seems to be building and the drawing routes to the jack are beginning to be blocked, it is sometimes wise to take the bull by the horns and take positive action fairly early on in an end, especially if you are well placed at the back.

If, in a fours game, the jack is still accessible with weight when your number three is on the mat, he can try a timing-shot in the hope of picking up the jack and burying it in the ditch behind the pack of front woods – which were once the head. Of course, if he misses the jack, there may be other alternative targets that might pay dividends.

I have even played the shot in singles many times, and it is the sort of shot which can really swing a match in your favour, although it is not likely to be too popular with your opponent. If you miss, you may be in trouble, but once you have decided to play the shot you must not stop to consider the possiblity of missing. Think positive, and you will be rewarded. Belief in the shot is very important.

The timing-shot wick

We saw what a wick was on page 66, but a wick obtained using a yard of weight is very different from a wick at speed, courtesy of a firm timing-shot. Such a cannon-ball can inflict a lot of damage, and can be deliberately played indirectly.

The jack itself, it must be admitted, is a small object to hit at 40 yards (36 m). Much better, then, to go for a bunch of woods, especially if there is a good chance of bouncing off them-effectively using them as a wall.

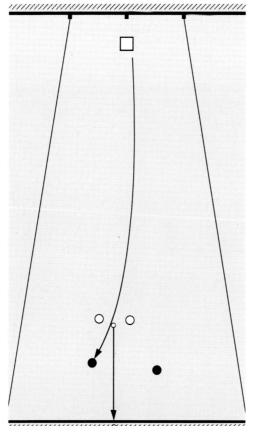

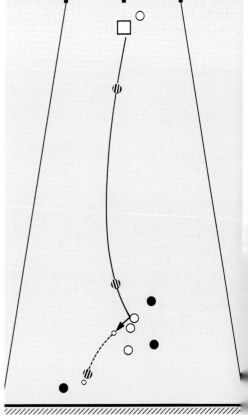

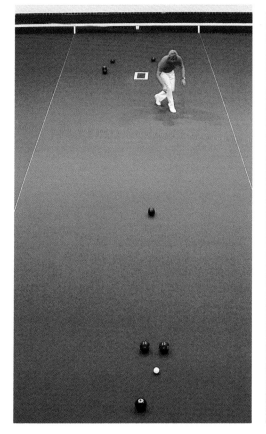

The classic split is a very satisfying shot to play. Get it right and your own bowl stays in the head, but controlled weight is called for.

The split

The split is another gift to the timing shot. Two bowls lying across the rink, close to each other, not touching but without enough space in between them for a bowl to pass, offer a target some 15 inches (38cm) wide. A whole foot (30 cm) wider than a solitary jack. Most bowlers would surely bet on themselves hitting such a target.

But there is a substantial bonus, for if a firm wood strikes the target pair anywhere near the centre of the target, the result is predictable. Out will go the two bowls, one to the left and one to the right, leaving the striking bowl to follow through to some extent and do more damage, but gently!

The result may well be a jack pick-up and trail, with a degree of finesse you would hardly expect from a timing shot. A good example of how the controlled weight shot can be made to work for you, especially where the intelligent use of woods in the head is concerned.

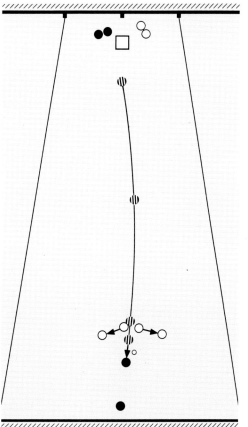

❝David Bryant played the classic split on the last end of the World singles final against Willie Wood at Auckland in 1988. On that occasion, David was two down in the head, and the score was 22-all, so he had to take firm action. His response was to fire, and, although he took out the two scoring bowls, his own bowl sped through to the ditch. If David had used a timing-shot, he might have kept his own bowl alive.

I'm not criticising his choice of shot, for he played the all-out drive because a) he was desperate, and b) he was in New Zealand. And of course, his tactics worked, for he fired again with his next bowl, winning the match and the World title.❞

THE TIMING-SHOT: THE FLYING JACK

Firm woods can do a lot of damage, and that is why, more often than not, they are used. Sometimes they can be employed as a means of insurance against disaster when a potentially profitable gambit is being played.

For example, you might see some future in attempting to take out your opponent's shot because you have three seconds. Then you notice that if you play the shot with a yard-on delivery, which is the obvious and neat way of doing it, you take the risk of brushing the jack in passing and flicking it towards three of your opponent's bowls.

You can minimise the danger by playing what would normally be considered the more adventurous shot, with a lot of weight. If you play it with a firm timing-

shot, it can still go wrong, of course, but if it does, the jack is likely to fly.

A killed end is a much better proposition than going three down, and, remember, there is still a fighting chance of coming out of it with four for yourself! Oddly enough, a heavy bowl can be safer tactically than a dead draw at times.

ALLCOCK'S TIP

● *If you think of the timing-shot as a draw rather than a drive you will find selection of weight much easier. Say to yourself, 'If this bowl were to be unobstructed, where would I want it to finish?' Then play it as a simple draw to that position.*

1-4 If things could go wrong, don't be half-hearted. Play with enough weight to ensure that the jack will go dead.

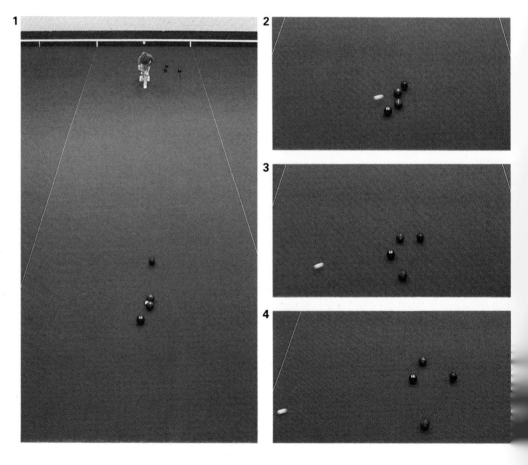

THE TIMING-SHOT: USING THE SWING

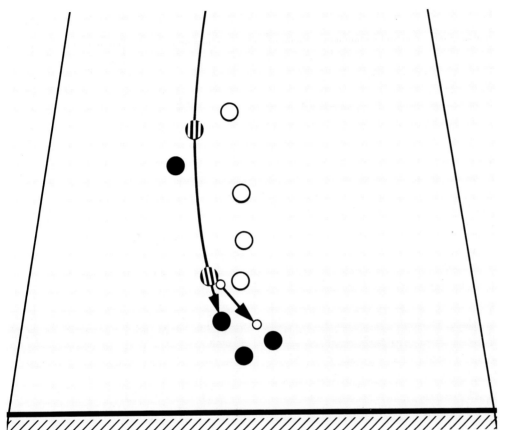

❝ Not only does the swing of the timing-shot allow you to get around obstacles, but it gives you the opportunity of getting into a pack of enemy bowls at an angle. The effect can be similar to hitting a skittle at an angle in the 9-pin alley game which is played in so many pubs in rural parts of England. That is the way, skittlers tell me, to get a strike, or a spare, by knocking all the pins down in one fell swoop. ❞

Left: If there is a short bowl stopping the drive, you will need to use the timing-shot to 'swerve' around it.

If you decide you ought to attempt to hit the head, you might find that the firing line – the direct line to the jack – is blocked, either by our opponent's or by your own short bowls. If you have the timing-shot in your armoury, however, there is no problem – you can use less than firing weight, and skirt around those blockers, probably gaining more control into the bargain.

The timing-shot is a compromise shot, but there are times that you can be grateful that it is possible to combine firm weight and a fair degree of swing. So, when you feel inclined to use weight, don't jump immediately to the ultimate weapon – the drive. Stop and consider whether a timing-shot would be more appropriate.

The timing-shot might give you the chance to approach the head at a more advantageous angle – sometimes that can make all the difference. And, of course, if you are versatile enough to vary your line and weight so that you can play all the shots, it will be extremely difficult for your opponent to block you out.

If you demonstrate that, wherever he places a blocker, you have the ability to dip inside it or skirt round it by varying your weight, you will affect his confidence considerably. Think how often you have seen David Bryant 'get out of jail'. His escapology rivals that of Houdini, but his secret is simply the wide range of shots in his repertoire.

As with previous shots, this is one to practise. Set up a head which needs hitting, and place some blockers in the firing line. Play the controlled weight shot to swing round the blockers until it becomes a natural part of your game.

THE TIMING-SHOT: USING THE RIGHT WEIGHT

'Often it does not matter what weight you play as long as you hit your object, but sometimes the weight required is critical. Analyse the head, and decide if there is an optimum weight for the shot, and, if there is, be explicit when asking your second or third to play it. If you are playing the shot yourself, be sure you do not get carried away by your enthusiasm to hit the target: concentrate on giving your bowl exactly the right weight. '

When weight is called for, does it really matter how much weight you use? Isn't it simply a matter of the more the better – as long as you maintain accuracy?

Yes and no. Yes, it does matter how much weight you use. And no, it certainly isn't a matter of the more the better.

There are times when, although you are a shot or shots down, and you need to take positive action to remove them, the last thing you want to do is to smash into the head indiscriminately. You may have too much to lose: perhaps have only one wood in the head, and might risk dropping a count; or perhaps you have built up a good position, with lots of woods in the head, and you would like to exploit it.

Either way, you don't want to sacrifice your own woods, which disaster would be quite on the cards if you were to use all-out

firing weight. In this case, using the right weight is vitally important, and you must learn how to decide what the optimum weight is, and be able to deliver the bowl with the correct strength.

Unfortunately, too many players show an inadequate grasp of the principles behind the choice of weight, and too easily resort to an indiscriminate blockbuster every time they are in trouble. 'Two or three yards of weight' suggests the skip. 'Whoosh!' is the response, as the bowl rockets into the ditch.

Make a promise to yourself to be more accurate when describing the weight you are going to use or are asking your team-mates to use, and make a point of practising these in-between weights called timing-shots until you can be more precise in using them.

1-4 Sometimes things could go wrong if you use too much weight. Again the timing-shot comes in useful.

1

2

Swinging with weight

On most greens there is one side of the rink which swings more than the other on a drawing line. Normally that side of the rink will swing more with weight as well. Take that as a general rule only, for it isn't always the case.

I always like playing my timing-shots on a swinging hand, for I feel I can depend on the natural swing of the green to bring my bowl back into the head. A straighter hand often is much less reliable, tracking out with weight in a way that is difficult to predict.

Bowls is all about bias, and I like to see my woods working for me, and when I can guarantee a good swinging hand, a well-judged timing-shot can be a joy to play. A lot of bowlers tell me how difficult the shot is, but, without wishing to appear immodest, it has always come naturally to me.

If you find it difficult, I am sure you will improve with practice – it is precisely the difficult things that should be practised more than those you find easy. But, so often, what practising goes on seems to be aimless, with little or no attempt to get to grips with any specific problem or skill.

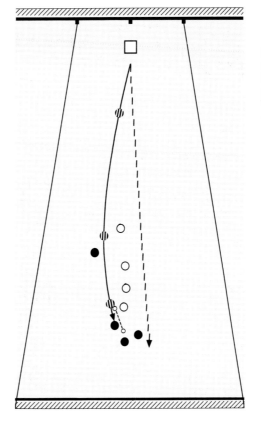

If you decide to use weight, the swinging side of the rink is often the better bet – it is more reliable, and less likely to track out against the bias. You know for certain the bowl will bend!

3

4

‘ Bowls is all about bias. Whether you are drawing or playing a shade of weight, it is a joy to see the bowl bending. By the same token, it fills a bowler with dismay to see his bowl catch a run in the green and 'track' straight past the jack. Such behaviour is unnatural. A good swinging hand is *made* for the timing-shot. Watch your bowl bend predictably. It's a shot you will be able to master in no time at all – given that good, reliable swinging hand. ,

FIRING: A VALUABLE WEAPON

❝I see experienced bowlers firing at the wrong time; I see young bowlers, aggressive by nature, firing too often: but no-one can deny the desirability (even the necessity) of having the drive in your repertoire. ❞

The most dramatic shot in bowls – the firing shot or drive – stimulates more controversy than almost any other aspect of the game. People are divided into those whose imaginations are fired by the drama of accurate and sudden destruction, and those who disapprove of what they consider to be an act of sheer vandalism.

'It takes an artist to paint a picture', I have heard it said, 'but any vandal can destroy one in no time at all!' This is a point of view, I suppose, but firing is so much part of the modern game that no player can be said to be completely kitted out until he has learnt how to use the big gun.

Firing is not easy, nor cheap. Most of the criticism comes from people who imagine it is. Often, if you miss your target by a fraction of an inch, you achieve nothing, and, seeing that you probably wouldn't be firing at all unless you were in trouble, a miss could be expensive.

Neither is firing the domain of people who can't draw and prefer to be heavy-handed. Think of men whose fast and accurate firing has made them famous. Bryant, Belliss, Baker and a young Scotsman named Angus Blair drive fast and fearlessly, yet they are also among the best touch players in the game. I am sure that all four would claim to win more matches through their drawing ability than through use of the firing shot.

Firing, then, is a vital skill, as is the ability to use it with discretion. As with so many other skills and techniques discussed in these pages, knowing when to resort and when not to resort to it is just as important as mastering the skill itself.

When you have mastered it, however, your game will have another dimension. Even if you never use the shot in a match you will be a more confident player knowing that you have 'last line of defence'.

1-4 Fire at a wide head to reduce the count if you are several shots against. You might even get a bonus – if they are arranged favourably, they might all go out, as they did for me on the end illustrated. Notice how one of my bowls – to the left of the jack – remains undisturbed and ends up shot.

The excitement that reverberates around a green when one of the top players is about to unleash a thunderbolt testifies to the entertainment value of the firing shot, and consigns the objectors to the role of old-fashioned stick-in-the-muds. But the true worth of the drive is not restricted to its entertainment value.

Firing to reduce the count

All forms of firing are intended to be destructive, but the most common reason for resorting to your 'last line of defence' is when you are a lot of shots down. You can hardly then be worse off.

Generally speaking, don't fire if you have a lot of room to draw a good saver – and don't feel you have to draw the shot itself. Firing is really a desperate measure that you undertake when your other options are not available, so do consider carefully whether a conservative draw wouldn't really be a better bet.

Generally speaking, don't fire if you are only one shot down – even if you have a couple of seconds. It's surprising what unexpected results can follow a firing shot. Maybe you might take your two seconds out and finish five down. Disaster! Even if

you accidentally removed only one of your close seconds, you may be handing a gift of an opportunity to your opponent to whip out the other one for a big count.

Most big counts I have seen – and I've seen a few eights scored in my time, even at International level – have been partially self-inflicted, and have involved one team helpfully assisting the other by obligingly removing some of their own woods with indiscreet firing.

Perhaps the most helpful advice I can give regarding firing is to do it rarely, but, when you do, make sure you hit! I'm sorry if that advice has an ironical ring to it, but I can do no better!

ALLCOCK'S TIP

● *Those people who abhor the firing shot can take comfort from what I said on page 54 – that a good drawer will beat a good driver any day, if he sticks to the draw and is not shaken out of his rhythm. As a one-off means of getting out of trouble, however, the drive is indispensable. Practise it assiduously.*

❛ Don't fire because you are *desperate*. Fire because it is the *best* shot to play in the circumstances. If there are seven shots against you, the head is three feet wide, and there is no road in to the jack on a draw, then the right shot to play is a drive. The idea is to take out as many shots as possible, so, normally, it will be a case of the firmer the better, as long as you are able to maintain accuracy.

This you might not do if you go at it too hard, or if you are so anxious about the prospect of dropping a count that you lose your bottle. Take care, take your time, but try to play the shot naturally, just as though you were not under any pressure at all. Of course, I *do* know it's not as easy as it sounds! ❜

3
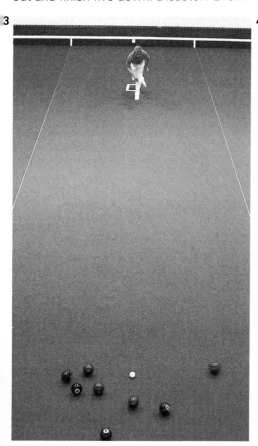

4
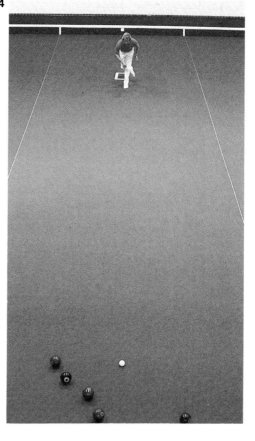

FIRING: KILLING THE END

' Again, it is important to relax and fire naturally, having confidence in your ability, which you have honed through practice. You know *you are a good firer, so why allow the tension of an adverse head to affect your accuracy? It's mind over matter – like everything else in bowls! '*

There are ends where you get into trouble from the start, maybe because of tactical error, or perhaps your technique has let you down. A succession of short woods is more likely to be a result of bad play than bad tactics. By the completion of the end, you are in so much trouble, with no position, that your only chance is to put the jack off the rink.

This is not a time to consider the timing shot: you need to generate as much speed as possible, so the jack will go the distance, over the string, even if there are a few ricochets en route. Be careful, of course, to keep control and keep all your movements in a straight line, as suggested earlier, so that you do not sacrifice accuracy for speed.

Don't strive for perfection if there are woods in the head. Desperate measures are called for, and, as long as the shot is effective the means of achieving it are of secondary importance. Practise the shot, though, to improve your accuracy, for there may be a time when you have to make a dead end and have only a single bowl or – worse still – only the jack to hit.

When you are desperate, go for the kill. Use maximum weight to make sure that the jack will go dead.

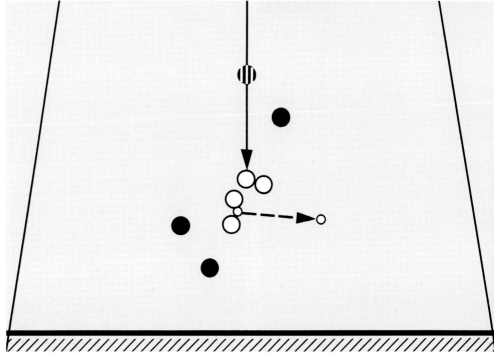

Firing at a single bowl

There is one situation where firing is *not* a last resort, for it can be used as a safe way of taking a single bowl out of the head, or ditching the jack when you are already holding shots.

When you are performing a take-out of a single bowl, or maybe attempting to remove two for the price of one, it would be normal to use just enough weight to accomplish the job – pushing the offending wood or woods far enough to bring your own into the count, but no further.

However, using the 'correct' weight might lead you into dangers you hadn't anticipated. For example, the track you have to take might bring your attacking bowl near to the head or near to a bowl that could be pushed into the head. Then, for once, it might be safer to use more weight rather than less, especially if you are confident about your firing ability, and confident about the hand you decide to play. This is a time for firing on the swinging hand, for the reasons suggested in connection with the timing-shot on page 75.

The reason that a drive would be safer than a firm, running delivery is simple: the drive takes a road well away from the head or any dangers associated with the head, and, as long as you are not going to be a foot or so off target, the shot is perfectly safe.

If you are liable to be a foot or so off target, I suggest it is time to practise the shot, along with all the others. You may need it one of these days.

Ditching the jack

The same thing also applies to ditching the jack under certain circumstances. Imagine you have trailed the jack to within inches of the ditch, and your toucher has settled in front of the jack, or maybe by the side of it.

In this position, your opponent has a chance of retrieving the shot with a good delivery. You can take the chance away from him by ditching the jack – and maybe the toucher as well – and put the result of the end virtually beyond doubt.

A yard-on might do the trick, a timing-shot would probably be better, but a firing shot could be the safest or easiest to play in the circumstances. There's no right answer, for every end is different. but it's worth thinking about.

When going for a single bowl, or the jack, you have to be even more accurate. Build yourself up for it this time, 'previewing' your success in your mind, but allow yourself, if possible, to play the shot without pressure. I find I am so successful in building myself up for the single-bowl take-out that in fact I am more likely to get what I am playing for than if I were going for a bigger target.

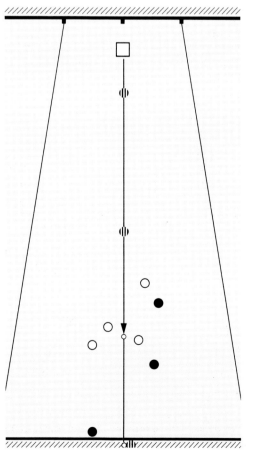

Far Left: Firing can be safer than the timing-shot when going for an isolated bowl. Play it with confidence.

Left: You can fire confidently for the jack if it is surrounded by your opponent's shots. If you don't get the jack, you are likely to reduce the count.

OMITTING TO PLAY A BOWL

❝ Don't be over-ambitious. Especially in a team game. When your team-mates have striven to get the shot, showing skill and good temperament under, perhaps, difficult circumstances, why risk giving it all away? Quite apart from the effect on the scoreline, think what it could do to the morale of the rink! It's a mark of an experienced player to accept his own limitations, and his potential fallibility. ❞

Perhaps you can't imagine throwing a bowl away. Perhaps you regard it as 'chicken' not to 'have a go'. But there are times when discretion is the better part of valour. Sometimes, even when you are shots down in the head, it is wise to forego your right to play your last bowl of the end.

In fact it is only the final delivery of the end that you are allowed to jettison according to the Laws of the Game, and it was only fairly recently that a change was made in the Laws to permit it, after a

Right and Far Right: ''I wonder if I dare risk it?'' ''I'm not daft — one to you!!''

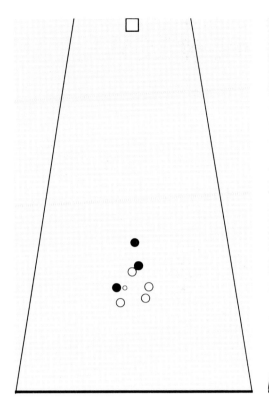
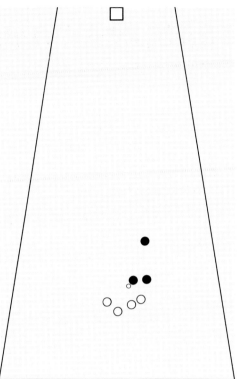

Positions where it might be best to accept the 'bird in the hand' and not to bowl a final delivery.

controversial incident in the World Championships at Worthing in 1972, when a team from Fiji were made to replay an end for omitting to play their last bowl. It cost them the match.

Ironically, the Law could have been proved to be a nonsense, for it has always

been possible to 'throw' your bowl at any stage of the end – not just the final delivery. All you have to do, if you are afraid of doing damage, is to fire your bowl into the ditch, bowl a wrong bias on purpose, or, safer still, deliver it short – even to less than the minimum legal distance of 15 yards (13.7m) so that the bowl is declared dead!

Illustrated here are some of the occasions that might cause a player to make the wise decision not to play his final delivery. Look at each one carefully, and see if you can spot the dangers for yourself. What would you do?

I have seen one of the world's top singles players examine a head in which he was already two shots down, turn to his opponent and declare his fourth bowl dead. That takes some courage, but could it be that the very unorthodoxy of the gesture would impress the opposition? Perhaps it might lead him to think 'What confidence! He thinks he can afford to give me two shots, and still beat me'.

One of the main factors that come into play in most of the potential last-word situations is the back position, and perhaps it is a good time to reiterate and emphasise the importance of building a head so that you are never put into an impossible position.

TEAM PLAY: THE FAMILY AT WAR

❛Four brilliant bowlers do not automatically make a good rink. At every level of the game, what you need are four team members who will pull together. There is no room for the prima donna in any rink, or in any team. If bowls, as we have said, is all in the mind, team morale is more important than sheer skill when it comes to the crunch.❜

One of the commentators at the World Championships at Aberdeen in 1984 suggested that the English four were more like a family than a team, because of the way they played for each other, rallying around if there were an emergency, and celebrating together after they had won the gold medal.

I was proud to be the skip of that four, and can confirm the family feeling that we shared, George Turley, Julian Haines, John Bell and myself, although at times I would describe it rather more graphically as a 'Family at War'!

I mean, of course, at war with our challengers from the other countries, not a war among ourselves. The comradeship on that rink was, I believe, the finest I have ever experienced on the bowling green.

I mention it because it is my firm belief that compatibility is the key to the success of any team effort, far more important than sheer ability, or solo brilliance. Four

outstandingly gifted individuals are not likely to make a good team unless they respect and like each other.

The unity among the players in England's young Hilton Trophy side that has won the Home International Indoor Series for the past five years or so is another example of success following good team selection which takes account of blend as well as raw talent.

It is a pleasure to play in the team, for you get the impression that everyone, including the officials and selectors, are rooting for each other. The pre-match pep-talks and post-match celebrations are all part of being a team, and being a family.

Perhaps it is a good time to stop and look at the family roles played by the respective members of a four, but whatever individual tasks they may have, none is quite so important as the player's contribution to the dynamics, the morale and general well-being of the family.

There was a wonderful team spirit about the England squad in world bowls in Auckland in 1988. Left to right: John Ottaway, myself, Wynne Richards, John Bell and David Bryant were all delighted to come home with gold medals and the Leonard Trophy for top team.

TEAM PLAY: THE LEAD

❝ You don't have to be a zombie to play lead, but you do have to be a very dedicated bowler. I have every admiration for John Ottaway, of Wymondham Dell, and Brett Morley, of Nottingham, two outstanding young England players who specialise in that position, and are feared throughout the British Isles. ❞

John Ottaway of Wymondham Dell: A quiet, patient man, admirably suited to his specialist position at lead.

In a four, the lead's task is to bowl his team's first two woods. His objective is simple: to get them as close as he can to the jack. If only it really were as simple as that, there would be no more to be said. In fact, his job is very difficult.

Firstly, of course, he has to concentrate on bowling close to the jack without any woods in the head to help him. You might say, by the same token, he has nothing to block his path, but it really is an exacting duty, ploughing the first furrow, as it were.

Secondly, he knows that the lead builds the foundations, so he is aware of the heavy responsibility that rests on his shoulders. If he misses in his objective, a lot more pressure will be thrown on the second man, who will not be expecting to have to play lead *and* second.

Thirdly, he must, if possible, try to find a perfect line, above everything, for the fine positioning of his bowls is going to make life more or less difficult for the other side. One in front and one behind – on a perfect line – is far better than two good length bowls, one a foot away to the right and the other a foot away to the right.

Fourthly, he must be of a patient and placid disposition, for he has to suffer the frustration of seeing his good bowls knocked to blazes as often as not, and never is he given the opportunity to respond in anger with a firing shot of his own.

Fifthly, he must often be the quiet man of the rink, who bowls his woods and retires into the background for ten minutes or so while the end he has started is completed and it is his turn once again.

John Ottaway, from Wymondham Dell, who led for me in the Fours in Auckland in the Sixth World Bowls Championships, fits the bill admirably. How he does it, I don't know – I know I couldn't be so patient!

TEAM PLAY: THE SECOND

The second's job is to deliver the team's third and fourth bowls each end, make up for the inadequacies of the lead when he fails, add shots when he hasn't, and have an eye to position, as directed by the skip.

Short bowls from the second are rarely useful, but woods through the head always are, so the second must remember to reach. He also has the duty, laid down for him in the Laws of the Game, of keeping the scorecard – carrying it on his person at all times – and checking it regularly with his opposite number.

Again the job description is easy; living up to it has its problems. On the whole,

though, it is a relatively comfortable position to occupy, for there is (it would seem at first sight) less responsibility than that carried by the back-end players, and the shots you are normally asked to play are nicely varied, but not so much as to put you off your length.

In fact, as any top player will tell you, the number two position is one of central importance to the rink. Just have another look at the opening paragraph, defining his role, and you will see that, if the second does his stuff, the four is well away, and the heads will be well set up for the third and skip.

Wynne Richards, the accountant from Troedyrhiw, who lives in London and plays for England, is one of the most effective seconds I know. He, too, was with us in Auckland, and made a typically gutsy contribution to our performance as a Four – not just with his woods, but with his morale-boosting sense of humour and perspective.

Many International seconds, like Wynne, are skips at club and county level, so they have to adjust to playing a seemingly subsidiary role. Some do it better than others, realising what a key role they are playing as number two. Others fail what I suppose is a test of character.

Many novices start the game at two and feel they are being promoted when they are picked at lead. They should forget any idea they may have about second being the position in which to hide – it is the anchor position of the rink.

Wynne Richards, the Welshman who plays for England: a great contributor to team morale from the number two position.

ALLCOCK'S TIP

● *David Bryant will tell you that he considers the number two to be the key player on the rink. He is the powerhouse, the workhorse, the anchorman, and has to be steady, versatile and reliable. At international level, most seconds are county skips, so they have an additional problem – adjusting to the unaccustomed role of taking orders instead of giving them.*

TEAM PLAY: THE THIRD

The third man has two woods, like his team-mates, and he delivers his team's fifth and sixth bowls each end. He is the skip's lieutenant – his aide – his deputy. He consults with the skip, giving advice and moral support, and he has to be able to play all the shots in a skip's repertoire.

He directs the head when the skip is at the mat, and is deputed the onerous duty of measuring for shot. The third is, in a sense, the skip's public relations officer, as he is in a position to keep in touch with the other members of the rink.

It is, for all those reasons, vital that the third and the skip should have a good working relationship, and especially so when considering the roles of the lead and the second. Imagine the disharmony that would result from a poor relationship at three and skip. The other two members of the four would have to make up their minds as to who deserved their allegiance. Mutiny!

The good number three will listen to his skip, give his advice, state his preference maybe, then wait for the skip to make his own mind up on all the evidence. Then, if the skip's decision is not in accord with the third's opinions, the dutiful lieutenant will not show dissent, but support his skip's decision to the hilt.

I have heard people say that a third and a skip should possess complementary qualities, so that, if a skip is known for his drawing, the third should be a good firer, and vice versa. Although there is obviously something in the theory, I would prefer both men to be versatile. In character terms, however, it works well if the skip is a quiet man, for an extrovert number three to provide the motivation.

John Bell was my number three when we struck gold at Aberdeen, and was there again, at my side, in Auckland, when we won the bronze medal. He is a classic third – as well as a formidable skip in his own right. He has all the shots – that goes without saying. And he is one of those men you feel you can rely on in an emergency: a good tactician, and a good motivator. What more could you want?

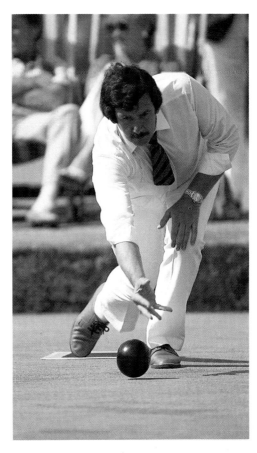

' A third, although he is often expected to play a 'skip's shot', will play it in a different frame of mind. Whereas a skip might play a shot with abandon, 'death or glory' style, because he knows there are no woods to follow, a number three may play with less weight, for example, so that his bowl, if he misses, will finish in a useful place and give the skip something to play for. A good third will think unselfishly. **,**

John Bell, the Cumbrian Cowboy: plays all the shots, and is a most supportive third man, always full of encouragement for the skip.

ALLCOCK'S TIP

● *There's a lot more to playing third than a lot of people realise. It goes without saying that you need to be an all-round player, but your major contribution is one of support for the skip. Playing third to a stranger, as you might be asked to do in a trial, is a hit and miss affair.*

Preferably you should know the skip pretty well off the green as well as on it, so that you can build on your personal relationship. You have to sense when to draw your skip's attention to something and when to remain silent. You have to sense when your skip is in need of some words of encouragement, and when he is best left to himself.

TEAM PLAY: THE SKIP AND HIS ROLE

 The skip is the conductor, in charge of his orchestra. He has to know the score, and his musicians, and he has to have a clear idea where he is going to lead them. There is one difference: the skip is actually sitting alongside his players, and hopefully playing the same tune!

Playing skip, especially for England, is a responsible job. Not only do you have to play all the shots, but you have to be a tactician, a psychologist and an expert in man management.

The skip is the captain of the Four. He delivers the seventh and eighth bowls for the team, and controls tactics and men, so he must be good at making decisions and at the art of man management – as well as the comparatively simple task of playing bowls.

The skip has to be able to play every shot in the book: draw; yard-on; timing-shot; and drive. He may come up against new situations, with which he must be able to cope, technically and temperamentally. He will be expected to save his side when they are in trouble, and add shots mercilessly when they are not.

An inspirational role
He will be more than pleased if his men give him such an armchair ride that he merely has to tidy up and put in a positional bowl now and again. And part of his job is

to encourage them to do just that. He may do this by example, or he may simply inspire them.

The greatest skip I know for getting the best out of his men is Mal Hughes, from Hartlepool, who, without bowling a bowl, can galvanise his men and talk them, cheerily, into giving of their best. Make no mistake, he can play a bit himself, but I am referring chiefly here to his inspiring personal qualities on the green.

David Bryant, too, is an inspirational skip, both in the non-stop encouragement he gives his men, and in his magical play. A man who is capable of escaping from impossible corners has got to be a tonic for the morale of his team.

One of the best things a skip can do for his men is to give them respect. Even at International level, where every bowler is by definition a class player, that does not always happen. But, as 'head of the family', the skip has a duty to keep all of his men involved in the game, and to listen to any contribution any one of them has to make.

Some club bowlers believe that the third should not advise the skip on his first delivery, but should control the skip for his second bowl. That is nonsense. Both the skip's deliveries are his own, and no-one else's – so, for that matter, are the woods of the lead, second and third. The skip carries the can, and all tactical decisions are his.

However, no skip worth the name would ignore advice, wherever it comes from. Even the humble second's opinions are worth listening to. In a good four, when there is trust and harmony, everyone has his say – but it is the skip who finally makes the decision.

One last thought: it is the skip's name that gets published when the results reach the press. It is a measure of responsibility that he is always glad to take when it comes to the credit for a good win. Of course he can be very generous and share the publicity with his men when the rink goes down!

Peter Brimble of Bristol: an astute strategist and highly experienced English international skip, in recent years best known for his inspirational management of England's indoor side.

Non-playing captains and managers

So far we have looked at team play as if the team were a team of four. In the Home International Series, which are still, for British bowlers, the highlight of the indoor and outdoor seasons, the nations are represented by teams of five rinks (outdoor) and six rinks (indoor).

Each national team has a Captain, who may or may not be a player, and it is customary for there to be a Team Manager as well. These are the officials who look at the overall game plan, and are in touch with the end-by-end developments as each match unfolds.

The role of both Captain and Manager is again inspirational, but there is a more down-to-earth side to their jobs, partly statistical and partly strategic. In England's indoor set-up at present, Peter Brimble and John Wiseman hold the posts of Team Manager and non-playing Captain respectively. Both are former international players.

The two officials keep an eye on the main scoreboard, and on individual rinks that may be struggling and could do with some encouragement, and when the scores get tight overall, they discreetly keep the players informed of developments and suggest strategies for attack or defence.

They also provide things like orange juice, biscuits, and news of the latest football scores. Trivial? Not at all! Such things are very important.

Tactically, a person with a game-wide view is able to advise caution or adventure, according to the circumstances. At Swansea in 1986, on information received from the bank, an important sacrifice was made by my colleague, John Bell, whose four were in possession of a 100 per cent record in international matches.

Kept informed of the game score by the eagle-eyed Peter Brimble, John selflessly gave up the chance of retaining his unbeaten record, and played two positional bowls. These bowls ensured that Scotland could not score the three shots they needed to win the match. If John had been greedy, however, he could have slotted in two more shots for his four, and kept that unbroken record.

Good team play, as you would expect – and good monitoring of the situation by the England management.

‘ The skip's job is to encourage his players, and develop their confidence until they believe they can play the shots he wants them to. May I make a plea on behalf of the skip? There are times when he, too, is in need of encouragement, and it would be nice if his players could remember that! ,

THE SINGLES GAME: HEAD-TO-HEAD

The Laws of the Game used to state that the basis of the game is fours or rink play. I'm not sure that I agree with that assertion.

Although I accept that team spirit and cordiality are part of our sport, the basis of any game is surely found in simple head-to-head combat. There is something primitive about singles that the 'social' atmosphere of team play tends to disguise. To my mind, singles is pure bowls, both psychologically and technically.

Let's get it straight: I enjoy playing in and for a team, because there is something uplifting about being a member of a well-knit unit – especially one which is successful, like our England teams are at the moment. One of my most treasured memories will be collecting the Leonard Trophy for the best overall team performance at Auckland, with my colleagues, John Ottaway, Wynne Richards, John Bell and David Bryant.

But, there is nothing quite like the classic gladiatorial battle between one man (or should I say 'person') and another that you get in single-handed combat. It is no coincidence that it is the singles game that is more attractive as a television spectacle, and that bowls is only now (with the increased focus on singles) becoming acknowledged to be a good spectator sport.

I feel that singles players mature like a good bottle of wine. In my early days, I used to think I was a good singles player, full of bounce and confidence, and I had some success, winning the EBA Junior (Under 25) Singles three times.

However, my singles game deteriorated as I grew older, and I took more interest in team games – learning, I hope, to become a good team member, and to be more conservative in my approach for the good of the team.

It is only recently that I have returned to the game of singles, and given it my full attention – and I think my attitude to the game is much more mature than it used to be. My good friend, David Bryant, who has

been such a good influence on my career, commented the other day that he had noticed a new maturity in my game. It was kind of him to say so – and I must say I think he was right!

Certainly, if you look at my results, my recent wins in the Embassy World Indoor Singles, together with other big tournament successes, point to a tightening of my singles play. I don't honestly feel I'm a better player than I was – simply that I have developed a tighter control of my temperament, and learnt to be more conservative (but not *too* cautious!) tactically.

Over the next few pages I will try to recommend some tips I have found useful when playing singles. But, even if you follow them all to the letter, I'm afraid I can't guarantee you success. After all is said and done, when you have studied the green, the weather conditions and your opponent, when you have analysed the land, the line and the length, you will still have to come to terms with your own mental attitude to the game – call it temperament, will to win, or just plain 'bottle'.

Which hand do I play?
An old rule says: 'The shortest way to the jack is the best'. There's a lot to be said for it. Give the narrower of the two hands a fair chance, but, don't be afraid to switch to the swinger if the straight hand appears unreliable – as it well might (straight hands are often tricky, especially to certain bowls). In any case, once you have decided which hand you are going to play, keep to that side of the rink, forehand one way, backhand the other.

Playing on heavy greens
Always play to a long jack on the trial ends. This will give you a chance to encounter the *worst* that the heavy green can offer. Try a smaller bowl if you play a lot on heavy greens – the old lignum vitae bowls (real 'woods') were always good in the long grass! Once the game has started, try bringing the mat up the green to achieve

Far Right: Singles, rightly or wrongly, gets more media attention than any other part of our game. Here I am with the Embassy World Singles trophy I won in 1986 and 1987.

more swing on the worn ends of the rink, and to avoid 'hurling'. Above all, don't play 'neat' bowls – and be up to the head. Short bowls are useless!

Playing on fast greens
As the England team found in the World Championships at Auckland in 1988, the first thing you must do on fast greens is to slow your action down. If you are running through the head, try deliberately playing short. You will be surprised how far your bowl will roll. Bowling tight (on a narrow line) is a punishable offence on fast greens – always aim to overgreen your bowl, taking a wider line than you think you should. In New Zealand I found myself taking marks on the bank as my aiming point – which I have never had to do before!

Playing in the rain
I find playing in the rain is easy. Perhaps it's the practice we get in England! Seriously, greens quite often play better when wet, as the water seems to hold the surface together, and, although the pace of the green will usually drop, at least it will serve to standardise the pace of patches that may have been faster or slower when the green was dry. It's important to remain as comfortable as you can. Wrap a towel around your neck, wear waterproofs, of course, and use a chamois leather to dry your woods, and another towel to dry your hands. I use Surbowl to give me a more secure grip, but there are other gripping agents available.

Playing in the wind
To be quite honest, this is the one hazard I dislike most. It is the one element you can't predict or properly allow for – particularly if it is gusting. And a sudden gust can add two yards (2 m) to the length of your bowl, or, on fast surfaces, make a difference of five feet (1.5 m) of green. Take a tip from the golfers, and use a duster to ascertain wind direction, but, in a cross wind, once you have established the line, don't make any adjustments from bowl to bowl to cope with sudden changes in wind strength. Keep on bowling along the 'correct' line, and don't be put off by the odd bowl which is punished by the occasional gust or sudden lull.

Playing in the dark
In England, in the spring and autumn, we are often out on the green, finishing a game of bowls at dusk. Lights from the pavilion, cigarette lighters, matches, and even car headlights are pressed into service, and there is as much waving of white dusters and handkerchiefs as there must have been at Khartoum! To bowlers who wish to improve their ability to cope with playing in such conditions I would recommend a diet of carrots. But seriously, I always find it surprising that, difficult though it is, the standard of play rarely drops appreciably when darkness falls. And it is in the dark that my policy of 'natural orientation' comes into its own, and those who rely on marks on the green are often lost, for their landmarks are no longer visible.

Below: The artificial outdoor green at Greenacres Holiday Park, Porthmadog, is one of the fastest surfaces in Britain.

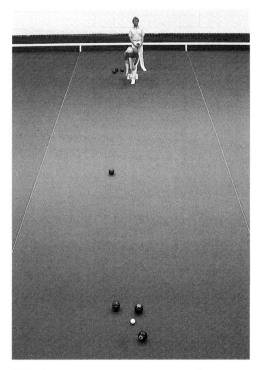

Few players deliberately infringe the law concerning possession of the rink, but there are a few bad sports aound. Here the default is simulated.

Playing on an uneven surface

Have a good look at your rink before you start to play on it, and pay particular attention on the trial ends. Make a mental map of the rink, so that you know, like a good card player, where every trick is to be found. Move the mat, when it is your prerogative, to avoid the bumpy patches or divots that might upset your smooth delivery. Remember where there will be bare patches, or the grass is sparse, and you may be able to use that knowledge to your advantage – these patches will play faster, and your woods will swing more as they roll over them.

Playing a 'difficult' opponent

Some bowlers, although they do not strictly break the Laws of the Game, can be difficult to play against. I am sure they do not always mean to be awkward, but their attitude, habits, manner or little mannerisms seem calculated to annoy. There are the moaners, the hypochondriacs, the inveterate talkers, and even more whistlers and singers, who, if you are not careful, will put you off your game. All I can say to you is: 'Believe in yourself. Play to your own strengths. Concentrate. As far as is possible, without being rude, ignore your opponent's idiosyncrasies. Be honest and straightforward, and play your own game, regarding any little difficulties as routine distractions to be overcome.'

Playing a bad hand

If at all possible, when you have detected a bad hand, leave it alone. Watch how your opponent's bowls behave on it, however, for you may be able to use the hand's tricks to your advantage if, for example, the jack is moved. Suddenly, the 'tricks' of the so-called bad hand may now lead you straight to the jack! Don't condemn a hand too early. There are bad hands and bad hands! A straight hand my look treacherous, but it may be reliably straight. The sort of hand you need to avoid is the one where there is no margin for error: a little too much green and your bowl does not come back; cut the green a fraction, and the wood whips away and finishes very tight.

Recovering from a bad start

Prevention, they say, is better than cure, but we have all fallen into the trap of making a disastrous start to the game, and it is important to have a survival strategy when that happens. Concentration is the answer. Be positive. Be patient. Don't panic. Calmly consider what your recovery tactics should be. What, for example, should you do with the mat and jack when next you win the shot? Disrupt your opponent's rhythm while trying to find a way of improving your own. Play every end as though it is the first, shutting out of your mind all your previous misfortunes. Don't 'go for shots'!

Concentration is vital. When I am concentrating properly, I am not aware of any possible distractions.

How to concentrate

This, I suppose is the $64,000 question. Remember that everyone has difficulties in this area. Everyone has his own natural and limited concentration span. Discipline yourself – be the master of your own destiny. Channel your thoughts and pull on your inner resources. Breathe deeply, and take your time. Don't talk to people on the bank, or allow yourself to be distracted. Train yourself into good habits, until you can believe in yourself and your own ability. And don't fall into the trap of concentrating on concentrating to the detriment of your game!

How to prepare for a big match

Preparation is a very personal thing. Some people need solitude in the build-up to a big occasion. Others prefer the re-assurance of social company. My rules before a big match are never to get involved in a business meeting, a traffic jam or an argument, never to take alcohol or go hungry. I might go for a swim, go window shopping, or relax and listen to music. I always like to get away from the venue, and often visit the Lake District when I am competing in the CIS UK singles at Preston. Think positively about the match, but don't be inflexible when it comes to a game plan.

You can tell a lot from your opponent from his handshake.

How to assess your opponent

As a general rule, it is wise, especially if you have never met your opponent before, to assume that he or she is the best bowler in the world! This is another way of saying: 'Don't underestimate him or her.' At the same time, there are some things you can look out for that can help you assess his strengths and weaknesses (I'll assume he's a man, as I usually play men). Where does he come from? Is he more used to bowling on a fast or a heavy green? Is he left or right handed? What bowls is he using? Is he a drawer or a firer? All these things can help you sort out a strategy for testing him on short or long jacks, and guide you concerning the advisability of packing the head with shots or putting in some insurance around the back!

Weaknesses to look out for

When the game gets under way, you will be able to ascertain whether your opponent has a preference for the forehand as opposed to the backhand, or vice versa. You will soon be informed by his body language if he is susceptible to pressure. Is he easily annoyed by his own bad luck . . . or bad bowling? Does he drive at the drop of a hat? Does he prefer long or short jacks? Try to remember any shortcomings, so that you may exploit them if you get the chance.

The ideal first bowl

It is much too simple to say that your first bowl should be as close to the jack as possible. Much has already been written on this subject, and there is considerable contention as to whether the ideal first bowl should be a front toucher or a back toucher. I would go for the front toucher, simply because, if struck, it will (or should) follow the jack into the ditch. A toucher that sits beside the jack, though skilfully delivered, is of little value – except as a rest for the opposition! On a very fast green, there is a lot to be said for the jack high bowl a foot (30 cm) or so away from the jack.

Moving the mat and jack

However well you think you are finding the rink, if your opponent is finding it better, you'd be well advised to have something up your sleeve. The favourite ploy is to take the mat for a walk up the green, and deliver a short jack to a full length position. This means that both you and your opponent

have to start from scratch as far as line is concerned, and, with luck, you will be the first to find it. After all, it is you who has called for the change, so you already hold the tactical initiative. It may be an old trick, but it is surprising how often it can turn a game.

Above: Taking the mat up the green is an old trick – but it often works.

Left: Is it better to have your first wood behind or in front of the jack? That's debatable – but it's great to have your first two fore and aft, and on the centre line of the rink.

PRACTISING WITH A PARTNER

A problem shared is a problem halved, they say, and it is good to have someone to work with when you are worried about some aspect of your delivery. A partner can help you set your goals, can assist in the management of the practice session, and can give an outsider's view of your delivery, often picking up a minor detail which you have missed.

First and foremost let me say that practising is not going out on the green and having a casual roll-up with your friends. I am not against doing that – far from it. I enjoy a friendly game. It helps me unwind. But it must not be confused with practice.

England's former Director of Coaching, Jimmy Davidson, is a firm advocate of what he calls 'purposeful practice'. As far as I'm concerned there is no other kind. Whether you are practising alone or with a partner, make sure you know what you are trying to achieve, and are setting about it methodically.

If you have a partner, it can help, for he can share in the routine duties of centring the jack, and setting up heads to practise various specialised skills. We have looked at many examples in this book.

I have a trick to help find the line, using a handkerchief placed on the green. It is, I reckon, easier to bowl over a handkerchief than it is to hit a line every time. The positioning and repositioning of the visual aid is really a two-man job. And you can learn from each other's critical comments – as long as they are constructive.

I do the same when I am practising driving. I prefer to place a mat as the target, first across the green, then lengthways as I sharpen up, until finally comes the test when I fire at a solitary jack. Again it makes things easier if you have a partner at one end to replace the jack when you are on target, and at the mat end too to add the spice of competition.

Your partner can add the contetitive edge during practice, and help to create the reality of bowling to changed heads, but don't get carried away with the game – you are out there to improve. Ask your partner to observe your delivery, and analyse it together. You don't have to be a qualified coach to use your powers of intelligent observation.

Don't be afraid to ask your club coach – if you have one – for advice. In England, he will have learnt his trade through the EBCS, and will know what to look for. If you are not scared of the prospect, ask him if he has access to video equipment. This is being used more and more as a coaching aid these days, and I know I learnt a lot watching my own action on television.

Right: Handkerchiefs may be used to mark the shoulder of the arc, as an aid to finding the right line in practice.

Far Right: A friend, coach or partner can share the duty of setting up heads for 'purposeful practice'.

PRACTISING ON YOUR OWN

If you can't find a partner, don't despair. Bowls is one of the few games you can practise on your own. It has that feature in common with snooker, darts, and athletics. Although you need opposition finally to test your skill in competition, you can develop and rehearse those skills quietly and privately in practice.

Even in the privacy of your own lounge – if you can get away with it – you can set a cushion up against the wall and practise your delivery without risking damage to your skirting board or room decor. And at the club, you can explain that is is not necessarily anti-social to practise on your own rather than get dragged into a triples roll-up for a pint on the next rink.

Try taking several jacks – as many as you can muster – and rolling those for twenty minutes. Good jack-casting practice; and a good way to monitor your control of both line and length.

Then, when you start on the woods, concentrate on the drawing shot – it is, after all, the basic shot in the game. Indeed, as I suggested on page 54, if we could look at every shot we attempt as a drawing shot we wouldn't go far wrong.

For a beginner, especially, it is important to master the draw before toying with any of the more complicated shots – the draw is complicated enough! So, draw, draw, draw, and draw again. When you think you have a fair idea of length or weight, you should try varying the length of the jack from end to end, or bowling to two or three jacks, all placed at different lengths during one end – perhaps using two or three sets of bowls.

For more advanced or adventurous players, look through this book and pick out those areas in which you have room for improvement, and try the ideas I have suggested. Try the different stances described on pages 21 to 29. Try different ways of finding the line, using marks of various kinds. Try the different ways of influencing length suggested on pages 46 to 53. And practise, not only in fair weather, but when it is wet and windy, too.

Practice is a time for experiment. Enjoy yourself. Try everything, but beware the trap of getting too confused. If you are not sure of something, go back to doing it the way it came naturally. The natural way is often the best, and it is the way I have always taken myself. I practise very rarely, preferring to rely on my natural ability, so it is a bit hypocritical of me to advise others to practise seriously.

I am sure however, that practise is essential both for the beginner and for the aspiring champion who wants to improve his game. So don't do as I do, do as I say. And, if you are going to practise, you must do so seriously and methodically if you are going to get anywhere. At the same time, however, don't take the game OR yourself TOO seriously.

ALLCOCK'S TIP

● *However helpful it is to have a partner, there are times when you are best left alone to concentrate on a particular problem, and give it your undivided attention. This kind of solitude can be good preparation for playing singles, for the total self-reliance that the singles game demands of you.*

One drawback – you will be practising alone, bowling bowl after bowl without interruption, and the continuity of this situation will not be repeated when it comes to playing in a match. It is an artificial scenario. In a real game, your opponent will be doing everything possible to break up the pattern – even slowing the game down to upset your rhythm.

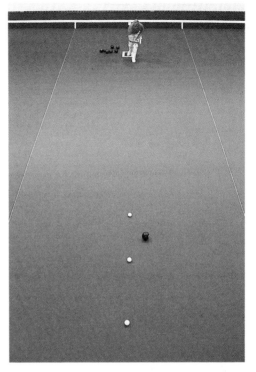

Try using three jacks for practising different lengths.

Bowls is one of the few games you can practise on your own.

RULES TO REMEMBER: THE LETTER AND THE SPIRIT

Every game has to have its rules and regulations. In bowls they are called the 'Laws of the Game', and help to keep the game moving more often than not. No code of Laws can possibly cover every eventuality, however, and I particularly like the foreword to the Laws of the Game governing Indoor Bowls, as they were first published in 1984:

'It is well . . . to remember that the Laws

How many bowlers know the laws governing touchers?

have been framed in the hope that true sportsmanship will prevail, and that, in the absence of any express rule, common sense will find a way to complete a happy solution to a knotty problem.'

Playing by the spirit as well as by the letter of the Law means using common sense as well as logic, and the long tradition of doing just that has led to the creation of unwritten rules, which I will deal with separately under the heading of Etiquette.

Knowing the Laws

I believe that every player should know the Laws of the Game thoroughly, but I suspect that even among top players there is a lot of ignorance. I am not suggesting that players should become more officious, or that they should start demanding their 'pound of flesh', merely that, if we take the game seriously, we owe it to ourselves and to our opponents to understand the day-to-day workings of the game.

It is largely through ignorance, for example, that bowlers contravene Law 50, which deals with Possession of the Rink. At the Superbowl, several of the crown green bowlers fall foul of this particular Law, but it is one which has no equivalent in their own code. Flat green players should not be able to plead ignorance, but too often a player is caught between mat and jack when his bowl comes to rest and possession of the rink passes to his opponent.

Personally, I feel that as long as my opponent is making good progress towards one end of the rink, he is not breaking the spirit of the Law, but, if he is dawdling, or even stopping in his tracks halfway up the green, he is in breach of Law 50 and should be challenged by the Umpire.

Footfaulting is another example which can help us to determine the difference between the letter and the spirit of the Law. Laws 27 and 28 are quite clear about the matter, as we saw on page 19, but we must ask ourselves why the Law was created. Obviously, if there was no such Law, a player taking his wood halfway, threequarters, or even all the way up the green, and placing it in the position of his choice could not be penalised as he would not be in breach of any rule.

The Law is not intended to penalise minor infringements that bestow no advantage, and Umpires are recommended to go easy on marginal offenders. Of course all bowlers should try to adopt a delivery that conforms to the letter of the Law, but it would be sharp practice on the part of a player who tried to officiously invoke this particular Law simply in order to 'get one over' on his opponent.

In televised events, it is part of the professionalism of the participants to acquaint themselves with the rules of the event, especially in those particulars which may differ from normal practice. In the sets game, for example, the right to deliver or to give away the jack alternates from set to set, and you need a good memory to keep aware of the position. That is all part of the game.

When marking touchers, how many of us remember that they should be marked *before* the succeeding bowl comes to rest? And do you know if it can become a toucher after it comes to rest? Look at Law 33 regarding 'Touchers', and at Law 34 if you want to learn more about marking them.

The Laws concerning displacement of woods and jacks, too, are interesting, and not well understood by most bowlers. Have a good look at Laws 38, 46, 47 and 48, and I think you will be surprised. The main thing to remember is that the offending team has no right to a say in the redisposition of any displaced woods. All the options – and there are several – are with the non-offending team.

Most bowlers I know, almost without exception, would take the sporting option and genuinely replace any displaced jack or bowl as near to the original position as possible. Let it be said, however, that a bowler who invoked his right to have a bowl removed from the green or to have an end replayed, would not be out of order, and the offending player who had been careless enough to perhaps disturb a back bowl would have no redress, and no ground for complaint.

Let good sportsmanship prevail! But do try not to disturb the head!

ALLCOCK'S TIP

● *Ninety-nine per cent of bowlers, in my experience, are proud to play truly in the spirit of our great game. And that makes it a real joy to play. The few bad sports are like the odd, isolated rain-cloud in a blue sky – they are the very rare exceptions that prove the rule. My prediction is that bowls will remain untouched by the modern craze for bringing acrimony, scandal and controversy into sport. Not even the media can spoil it – I hope!*

I believe that every player should know the laws of the game thoroughly. They are published in the EBA handbook – and at the end of this book too.

ETIQUETTE: MORE THAN JUST A GAME

'My Mother, Joan, who who was an England player, gave me some very good advice: 'Learn to lose before you learn to win.' Losing with good grace is the first lesson for any bowler – and bowls is the sort of game where even the very top players get a lot of practice at losing!

When you are beaten, the moment of disappointment for you is a moment of triumph for your opponent. Try to hide your true feelings, and share with him his pleasure. The pat on the back, the shake of the hand, the congratulatory word – yes, I know, none of us *likes* losing, but it will make *you* feel a *bit* better about it as well! '

Important though Laws are, they don't cover everything. Unwritten rules are the answer. The long traditions of bowls give the game a richness of ritual and formality, of custom and practice, which may be slightly old-fashioned, but is entirely charming.

Shaking hands before and after the game; the afternoon teas which break up friendly matches; the good grace as you applaud your opponent's good shots; the gritting of teeth as you mutter 'All the best in the next round!'; the stopping for a drink in the clubhouse afterwards when all your rivalry on the green is forgotten: all these are part and parcel of our wonderful game of bowls – though you won't find any of them in the Law Book.

Even in Australia – if you pardon my surprise – woods are lifted, polished, and handed to the opponent like a butler serving a good wine. This normal Australian etiquette is only occasionally observed in Britain, although it is not uncommon for the mat to be fetched and offered to the opponent.

Etiquette, it seems to me, is what you can do, beyond the Law, to contribute to your opponent's enjoyment of the game – in contrast to gamesmanship, which means doing anything within the letter if not the spirit of the Law to gain advantage, even if you ruin the game as recreation.

Watching a women's singles tie in the Weston-super-Mare tournament, I witnessed a prime example of good sports-

"Well played – all the best in the next round!" Even in the rarified atmosphere of the EBA National Championships at Worthing there is always a spirit of good sportsmanship.

womanship a couple of years ago. At 20-20, Lucy Brownlee, the England player from Middlesex, had bowled all her bowls, but her opponent had one to come, From where I stood it looked like a measure for shot, but Lucy sportingly stated she fancied her opponent's wood for shot, and actually advised her not to bowl her final delivery.

Of course, Lucy might have been forgiven for hoping that her opponent might have had an accident with her final delivery and kept quiet, but she spoke up honestly, lost the shot and the match, and crashed out of the tournament. What her friend, the formidable Mavis Steele, said to her afterwards, I shudder to imagine! But I was mightily impressed.

Honesty, I feel, even if it is not in your best immediate interest, is always the best policy. Be honest enough to appreciate your opponent's good play and to acknowledge when you've had a lucky wick. Actually, I concentrate so deeply during a match that I neither expect to applaud him, nor him to applaud me. But, if he does applaud, it is courtesy to at least

I believe in giving credit when my opponent plays a good shot – but I always try to beat it if I can!

acknowledge his gesture.

When counting up your shots, always leave it to your opponent to concede. DO NOT take your own shots out of the head yourself. And if you are measuring for shot or second wood, always offer the measure to your opponent before calling in the Umpire.

Always thank the hard working marker for sparing his time, and buy him a drink. But while on the green it is not wise to make too much conversation with the officials. Or, for that matter, with anybody else.

Be aware of the possession of the rink Law, and stand well behind the head (or the mat) when your opponent is bowling. Stand still, of course, and don't move until he has completed his delivery. Wait for his bowl to come to rest before starting your journey to the mat.

If etiquette extends to behaviour off the rink, perhaps I should mention fixing dates indoors for national competitions. With current demands for rink space, it is often impossible to play it by the book, offering two dates and waiting for a formal response. A bit of give and take is needed, as always.

GAMESMANSHIP: WHERE TO DRAW THE LINE

Compared with etiquette, gamesmanship is very much the other side of the coin. It involves doing the very thing that you think might upset your opponent, while keeping your actions carefully within, or at least on the fringes of, the Laws of the Game.

Excuses offered before the start of a match are, in my book, pure gamesmanship. 'I only entered this competition for the practice'; 'I'm not very well . . . I don't know if I'll be able to play'; 'I only hope I can make a game of it.' Such pleas fall on deaf ears as far as I am concerned.

Worse still are those things said or done during the game itself, with the intention of distracting, disturbing, or causing annoyance: ill-timed talking, coughing, sneezing, singing or whistling – or kicking bowls 'absent-mindedly' behind the player on the mat. I am certainly not paranoid about it, but they have all been tried against me at some time.

There are, of course, ways to annoy the person on the mat!

Visual distraction is another trusty weapon of the gamesmanship fiend: standing too near the bowler, so that he feels intimidated; failing to stand behind the mat or the head; moving just as the opponent is ready to bowl; using a hand-kerchief, or tying a shoe-lace at the far end, behind the head as the bowler is launching into his delivery. Again, it's all been done!

Fortunately there are not too many bowlers at any level who are prepared to sink to such depths, but those few who are seem to have made a lifetime's study of it. At top level, such behaviour is virtually unknown, although you will find examples of bowlers attempting to psych their opponents out of the game.

Expressions like: 'What bad luck you are having today'; 'Yes, that's a difficult hand – did you see that wriggle' and 'I don't think your bowls are helping you – they don't seem to suit this green!' are calculated to undermine confidence, but are conveyed in such a sincere and charming manner that no-one could possibly take exception. Even the best bowlers have been known to join in such a battle of wits, and it is normally taken in good part, accepted, and shrugged off.

Talking of behaviour that saps confidence, I have always thought that David Bryant's generosity when applauding a good opposition delivery is so sporting it's almost intimidating – especially when he goes to the mat and plays the perfect answer. Gamesmanship? . . . of course not! But it's all part of the Maestro's natural repertoire – part of his winning style.

It ought to be made clear that there are lots of tactics, within the Law, that are perfectly legitimate, and should never be confused with gamesmanship. I am thinking of those people who are slow players quite naturally, and whose delivery, perhaps, is painstaking and statuesque. They are not employing gamesmanship, but be on the look-out for those who slow down a game deliberately.

Those exuberant characters who like

Fussing around in the opponent's field of vision can be very distracting. Kicking bowls 'absent mindedly' behind the jack has been known to disturb a player's concentration.

running on the green, slapping their team-mates backs and making a lot of noise may earn criticism from those who run the stadium, but they are doing no wrong in my book.

Nor are those up-and-at-'em merchants who try to fire the opposition off the green. If you find their behaviour intimidating, that's your problem. The only way to beat them is to keep your cool and draw, draw, and draw again.

I have even heard bowlers who obviously don't know any better describe the tactic of bringing the mat up the green as gamesmanship. What nonsense! Again, the ploy may be used partly to intimidate, but it is completely fair and within the Laws.

I am proud of my sport – and especially proud of its traditions of fair play and good manners. Tactics I approve of heartily, but gamesmanship I deplore. There is no room for it in bowls, and it is significant that it seems to have played no part in the rise to success of any top bowler I can think of.

May it long continue to be so!

‘ Don't be intimidated by gamesmanship. Try to be honest and straightforward, while tactful and polite, and, if you feel your opponent is indulging in unsportsmanlike behaviour, ask him to stop. If he doesn't, call in the umpire. In doing so, you are not being unsporting in the least, merely proper and correct.

It is, of course, important to be courteous and discreet in the way you approach this kind of situation, because it is always possible that your opponent is unaware of what he is doing. Perhaps he is ignorant of the Law he is breaking; perhaps he *knows* the Law, but is breaking it unwittingly: at least you can generously afford to give him the benefit of the doubt, but there is absolutely no need for you to be disadvantaged as a result. ’

BOWLS ON TELEVISION

Television has had a huge impact on bowls ever since the BBC covered the 1972 world outdoor championships from Worthing. In the late 1970s, the Embassy world indoor singles at Coatbridge (the event moved to Alexandra Palace in 1988) became a televised event, and the Jack High tournament at Worthing, then the Kodak but currently the Gateway, was born.

Since then, the CIS UK singles has found a home at the Preston Guild Hall, and the Midland Bank World Pairs is contested annually at the Bournemouth International Centre, and both events receive extensive live coverage by the BBC.

Granada created the Superbowl, now sponsored by Liverpool Victoria Insurance for ITV in 1984, in their magnificent Stage One studio in Manchester. They have, under the direction of Paul Doherty, an imaginative approach to bowls, and I have been delighted to be part of their commentary team for the past few years.

Other ITV regions seem to be extremely interested. HTV for example, my local station, has presented a highly successful Pro-Celebrity event in which, with David Bryant, I played bowls and chatted with such stars as Emlyn Hughes, Chris Broad, Duncan Goodhew, Suzanne Dando, Bob Champion and Brian Jacks.

Television has revitalised bowls, and turned it, from a well-organised social pastime, into a sport which has captured the public's imagination, and achieved recognition at long last. So far, fears that the consequent commercialism would change the game for the worse have turned out to be ill-founded.

The few changes forced on bowls by television have served to smarten up the game, to give it more credibility, and to

The portable rink goes down anywhere, and is a very fair test of skill, even though the atmosphere generated in the big arenas – like London's Alexandra Palace – can be intimidating, especially in your first game 'under lights'.

begin to reward the most successful players for their skill. And that must be a good thing. Add, as a spin-off, the grass roots benefit from sponsorship through the four national associations, and television can be seen to have done bowls a very big favour indeed. The coloured shirts, the use of 'lollipops' to signal the current shots position, the development of the 'arena' concept as a result of introducing the portable rink, and even the slightly more controversial issue of 'sets' as a means of deciding a match: all these are dragging the game, far from unwillingly, into the crucible of modern competitive sport.

But, for all this emphasis on entertainment, competition, and professionalism, none of the intrinsic values of the sport has been sacrificed. I am proud to report that sportsmanship and fair play and mutual respect is at as high a level in bowls as it has ever been. Playing for money has not had the slightest effect on the behaviour of any top player as far as I can see.

Left: Big Brother is Watching You – David Bryant under surveillance in Worthing's Jack High Masters.

THE YOUNG ONES: YOUTH IN BOWLS

' My third win in the England Under 25 singles, in 1981, was achieved with a lot more difficulty than my previous victories in 1975 and 1977. This informed me that the standard of young players in England was on the up. Since then, the trend has continued.

It is a marvellous thing for the four home countries that there are now so many young bowlers challenging for top honours. The big difference these days is that a youngster of, dare I say it, my age (I am 32!) has perhaps been playing international bowls for twelve years (I was first capped indoors in 1976) and can be regarded as a veteran.

I certainly *feel* like a veteran at times, with people like Hugh Duff, Angus Blair, David Holt, Alan McMullan and Jason Greenslade around! '

I started bowling when I was about eight years old, though most of my games were played at home, with myself as the opposition. I used to play 16 bowls per end, sometimes bowling with my left, sometimes my right hand, and played for major titles and championships and even international matches – in my imagination!

My mother, Joan, and father, Ernie, were both fine bowlers (my mother played for England) and were very encouraging, though they never had to persuade me to show an interest in the game. I have always described myself as a 'natural born bowler', and feel I learnt a lot from my early championship encounters which were played out in fantasyland.

It was at the age of 17 that I made my first appearance in the EBA national championships at Mortlake in 1972, two years before they moved to Beach House Park in Worthing, the current home of the EBA. I represented Leicestershire in the Pairs, partnered by another seventeen-year-old, Paul Clarke, who was also destined to become an England player. The average age of the other competitors must have been around 50 – or more!

Imagine how I feel now, in my early 30s, often one of the oldest competitors among so many young challengers, and how David Bryant must feel after nearly 40 years at the top. Actually, I feel very pleased that bowls has become so accessible to young people, and can identify with their ambition and hunger for success.

Among the young men who are pressing for recognition, the one I would pick out, in England at any rate, is David Holt from Bolton in Lancashire, who beat me soundly in the final of the EBA singles championship at Worthing in 1987. Then only 20, he achieved the unprecedented honour of winning the England singles and pairs titles in one week.

Gary Smith, from Sunderland, is another very exciting prospect who was first capped for England in April, 1988, at the age of 26. With his modern hairstyle, he epitomises an increasingly with-it image.

He follows in the footsteps of other top England players who were discovered and capped in their early 20s and who are still playing in the national side: John Ottaway, David Cutler, Andy Thomson, Russell Morgan, Roy Cutts, Bill Hobart, Brett Morley, Pip Branfield, John Rednall, Danny Denison, and Gary Harrington are just a few of them.

Scotland, who seem to have taken second place to England in recent years, may be poised to make a determined come-back if the strength of their youthful bowlers' talent is a good guide. They seem to have struck a rich vein of young talent, following the promising showing of Richard Corsie of a few years back.

Since then, Richard's brilliance has been eclipsed by that of Angus Ogilvie Blair, who became the 1987 British outdoor champion at the age of 22, and, to some extent by the simpler skills of Hugh Hepburn Duff, who at 24 won the Embassy World indoor singles title in 1988, having reached the semi-final stage in 1987, thanks to his magnetic drawing to the jack.

Scotland also have David Gourlay, Jnr, who, in the opinion of his illustrious father, is the 'best bowler in the family'. He certainly has prodigious talent, but whether he will ever top the achievements of his gold medal winning mother and father is yet to be seen.

Ireland, who blooded several teenagers about ten years ago, are reaping the benefits today. Jim Baker and David Corkill were two of them. Now they have Alan McMullan, won the Irish singles indoors and out before he was 21.

Welshmen Steve Rees and John Price are not yet 30, but they are positively old men compared with Robert Weale, who represented Wales in the singles at Auckland when he was 24, having played in the Aberdeen world outdoor championships four years before, and Jason Greenslade, who was only just 17 when he wore the Red Dragon badge in the indoor International Series at Aberdeen in 1987.

Far Left: Hugh Duff, who won the Embassy World Indoor Singles title in 1988, aged 24, having reached the semi-final the year before.

Left: David Holt, who won the England outdoor singles *and* pairs titles in 1987, at the age of 20.

Rodney McCutcheon, who won a gold medal for Ireland in the fours at Auckland in 1988 at the age of 24.

BOWLS AS A CAREER

I'm delighted, of course, and very lucky too, to be earning my living from what others regard as a hobby, but, like all careers, it has its trials.

Living out of a suitcase, and spending days and nights travelling to and from far-flung venues, living fairly comfortably it is true but anonymously in hotel bedrooms, I wonder if the people who seem to envy me and my new career realise it is not all honey and roses.

Signing contracts is something I still haven't got used to, but my manager, Jock McNeil is a great help.

On 13 August 1987, I was still the Principal of an Adult Training Centre for the Mentally Handicapped in the Gloucestershire town of Stroud. On 14 August, I was a professional bowler. It had taken something like two years to make the decision to break with the security of my career in education and go for an adventure in the unknown.

That I was able to make such a move reflects the changes that have occurred within the bowls world in the past few years. I miss the routine and the rewards of what was my profession, for my job in the Cotswolds was in many ways a highly satisfying one – but there is no denying the excitement of closing one door for the last time, and opening another, through which lies . . . what? Only time will tell!

A career in bowls! I am indeed a lucky person to be able to earn a living doing what thousands do as a hobby. But, make no mistake about it, I regard my new career very seriously indeed, and am trying to use the extra time I now have at my disposal by responding to those invitations I had to refuse when I was still an employee of the Gloucestershire County Council, as well as exploring other avenues open to professional sportsmen.

I am also lucky to have a Manager – Jock McNeil – who is able not only to relieve some of the pressures by encouraging me when I am playing, but by involving me in a whole variety of other new activities, because he and I realise I would be foolish and arrogant to assume I could support myself through prize money alone.

Since I turned professional, I am pleased to say that I have not been aware of any great pressures, although the opposition is as tough as ever. In the first major professional event – Liverpool Victoria's Superbowl – I took part in after leaving the Stroud Day Centre, I was admittedly disappointed to turn in a poor performance and suffer a heavy defeat.

But, just as the bowls press must have been dreaming up headlines like 'ALLCOCK SUCCUMBS TO PROFESSIONAL PRESSURE' and 'ALLCOCK CAN'T STAND THE HEAT', I managed to win the CIS UK singles at the Preston Guild Hall, and proved that my Superbowl reverse was, as England's outdoor Team Manager, Mal Hughes, sings: 'Just one of those things!'

Looking back, I wonder now how I coped with the pressure of trying to do two jobs at the same time. I was travelling through the night, playing over the weekends, and using all my leave. A holiday was something I never had. My employers at the GCC were wonderfully understanding, but I was reluctant to push them to the stage where they would have to say 'No!'

So, here I am, embarked at last on a professional bowls career. And the way bowls seems to be going, I would imagine that others will follow me and take the plunge in the not too distant future, whether as a player or in related fields.

There are so many openings for a professional career when you look at other sports that have made it already. Coaching, promotion, fashion, mail order, journalism and player management: these are all fields in which there is scope for people with talent and a love of bowls.

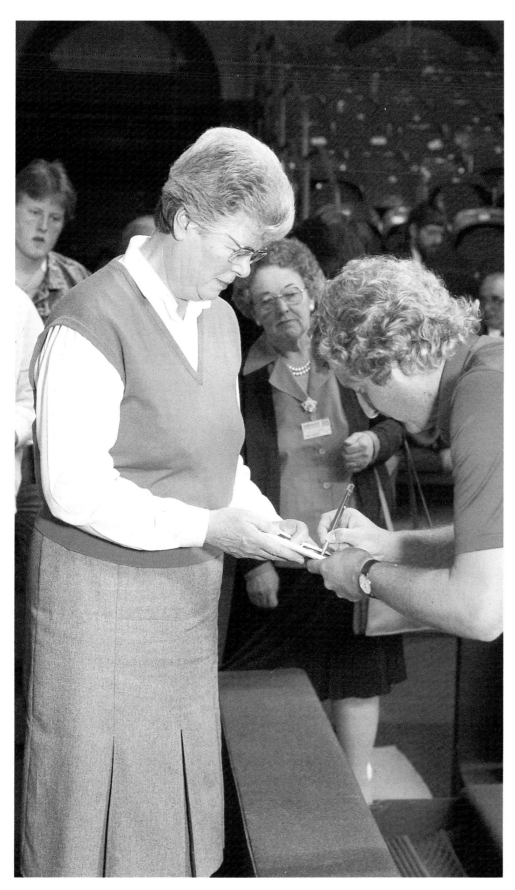

❝ Part of my policy as a professional is to safeguard a time to relax, when I can get away from bowls. For others, bowls is the hobby that allows them to relax away from their day job. For me, I need relaxation too, and I find it in music, reading, browsing in antique shops, or just walking and sight-seeing.

I recommend to anyone who is a serious bowls competitor the practice of getting away from the rink or the stadium in between games. Don't let bowls and bowlers suffocate you. Get some fresh air in those lungs. Re-charge those batteries. ❞

Signing autographs is all part of the day's work to a bowl's professional.

CROWN GREEN BOWLS

'There are a lot of things I like about crown green bowls, although I confess I knew little about the game until I spent a week – one of the happiest weeks of my bowling life – at the Crown Challenge at Blackpool in July, 1987.

I love the way in which the crowd is prepared to participate – and I mean noisily – shouting for their man. Even when they are to be heard shouting against the opposition, there seems to be no ill-will to it, and there is a superb atmosphere of great camaraderie.

I can't see the same thing happening at Worthing – except when the Middleton Cup finals are being played, and that's another great occasion! '

I always think that crown green bowling must be much closer to the historical game of bowls than our comparatively sophisticated flat green version. Bowlers in Shakespeare's day would not have worn blazers, nor played in serried ranks called rinks, and their rough and ready greens would have commonly been adjuncts to hostelries and public houses, like a lot of the crown greens in the Midlands and the North today.

That is the geographical limit of crown green bowling, apart from a lively overspill into North Wales and the occasional green provided for homesick holidaymakers in such places as Bournemouth or Spain. But, although it cannot be said to be a truly international game, crown green bowls has a tremendous following.

Crown greens used to be widely different – in shape and size – but are now designed in accordance with BCGBA recommendations to be reasonably standard, though standardisation clearly goes against the traditional grain, the majority of greens still defying anything that could be described as a norm. Oblong, irregular or even circular greens are commonplace.

The main feature of the game is the high point, or crown, between 6 inches and 18 inches (150 and 450mm) above the level of the perimeter. This crown need not be in the dead centre of the green, and, I'm told, on some crown greens there are two or more high spots.

Bowlers are equipped with only two bowls each, and the basic game is singles – although pairs is played from time to time. Triples and fours are unknown. With no rinks to divide the green, the ancient roving jack principle is employed, within certain limitations – there are currently no areas of the green where the jack may not be played.

Delivering the jack is called 'setting a mark', and the crown green jack itself may be black or white, is bigger than the flat green jack and is biassed – with the same number two (full bias) as crown green woods. (Flat green bowls have a number three bias and are slightly larger).

Whether delivering jack or bowls, the crown green player has to keep one foot in contact with the footer (the little round mat), so his back foot has to be anchored to the ground during delivery – which helps to explain the distinctive crown greeners' stance and delivery which I looked at on page 27.

Professionalism, new to level green bowlers, has long been associated with the crown code. 'Panel' bowlers have played for money for many years, and the crown green experts who have recently turned their attention to the flat game show a truly professional attitude and have been quick to learn.

Noel Burrows became the first crown ace to walk off with a major flat green title when he won the Superbowl in 1985, but there are others keen to follow his example, and many who are now playing the Association code indoors in the new EIBA stadiums in the North-west.

Above: The Waterloo Handicap at Blackpool is the Mecca of Crown Green bowling.

Left: There is less emphasis on standards of dress, and more rink-side gambling in Crown Green bowls.

BOWLING AROUND THE WORLD

My career in bowls has brought me the opportunity to travel, and it has been an education to soak up the culture of the places I have been privileged to visit.

Bowls, I suppose, originated in Britain, and as a great British pastime, commended itself to colonials throughout the Commonwealth, but, if you think we've got it taped in the United Kingdom, you'd be astonished to see the enthusiasm, organisation and quality of the greens in, for example, the southern hemisphere.

There were 23 countries playing in the world championships in New Zealand. Let me tell you about just two of them: Australia, the biggest bowling nation in the world; and Hong Kong, one of the smallest, but often one of the most successful.

There are more bowlers in Australia than in the rest of the world put together, they say, and my visits there have impressed me that if anyone has got bowls organised they have. I suppose their climate is ideally suited to bowls, but they certainly make the most of it, with multi-green centres and palatial clubhouses, especially in New South Wales, where the clubs are extremely wealthy, thanks to the income from their fruit machines.

Full-time professional greenkeepers with the very finest equipment keep the greens looking and playing immaculately, and cut and roll them constantly until they are 'polished'. This, together with the hot sun, means the greens are very fast indeed. Even the slowest Australian green that I played on was faster than the quickest I have ever played on in England.

For me, that meant lowering my delivery, cutting out body movement almost completely, and keeping my back foot steady in place on the mat until my action was complete. It also meant taking great care in the greening of the bowl to get the correct line. The swing is so vicious that the British player down under has to concentrate on over-greening the bowl rather than looking for an 'inside line'. Narrow bowls are cruelly punished.

Tactically, the Australian game is simpler than ours. The in-between shots we like to play in England, like the yard-on or the timing-shot are just too difficult to attempt. If you are not drawing, there is just one alternative: the all-out firing shot. There is no such thing as the percentage shot on those ultra-fast surfaces.

Heavyweight Australian bowls are the best for Australian greens. A small bowl is an advantage, because it seems to be less affected by windy conditions and is easier to control, because it has to make more revolutions to complete its course to the jack, and there is not quite such an urgent need to hold it back.

Although indoor bowls is virtually unknown, there is one fine stadium at Tweeds Head in Victoria, and it was a marvellous fillip for the Australian's carpet game when Jim Yates and Ian Schuback waltzed off with the Midland Bank World Pairs indoor title in England in 1987.

From the biggest bowling nation to one of the smallest: Hong Kong is one of the most competitive places in the world when it comes to bowls. The colony has fewer than a thousand bowlers, men and women, but has produced teams which have won five gold medals at world level.

Just look at this record:
Commonwealth Games: 1954 Fours, silver; 1970 Fours, gold; 1978 Pairs, gold; 1978 Fours, gold.
World Bowls: 1972 Pairs, gold; 1972 Fours, bronze; 1980 Fours, gold.

Perhaps the friendly rivalry that develops out of the intense social life in Hong Kong helps them to 'knit' and compete at world level. As I suggested on page 82, compatability is the greatest factor in team play, and our Hong Kong friends seem to have that commodity in abundance.

The greens in Hong Kong vary from good to not so good, and actually like ours in Britain, seem to vary in pace during the course of a game, which must make the home players very adaptable. The texture of the grass varies from a coarse-stemmed variety to a broad leaf, almost like a weed.

It was nice to see bowlers in white shorts and white socks, a very sensible form of dress in such a 'clammy', humid climate. Mixed bowling is encouraged, and

In Australia bowls is a
major national sport.

women seem to be given equal opportuni-
ties on the greens. Paying due respect to
the white clothing rule, one young lady
actually played one day in a white bikini.
Could it ever happen at Leamington Spa?

Bowls are played in exotic locations like
Fiji, Norfolk Island and Singapore. Bowls
are played in Japan, Swaziland and the
United States. Bowls are played in Argen-
tina, Zambia, Spain and Tenerife. Now that
the Sixth World Championships at Auckland are over, I for one am looking forward
to 1992, when England plays host to the
Seventh World Championships. What new
additions will there be to the growing list of
competing countries by the time top
players from all over the globe arrive at
Worthing for the World Bowls?

FEDERATION BOWLS

' Federation bowls takes me back to the happy days when I used to enter the tournaments at Skegness. What I learnt from the Federation code was the importance of drawing to the jack. Federation bowlers are deadly on the draw – as we have seen from those EBF bowlers who have come into the Association game and made their mark at international level. The latest of these is young Sally Franklin, who, at 23, has already won the EWBA 2-wood pairs title, and has been selected to play for England. '

Most bowlers in England play to the Laws of the Game as formulated by the International Bowling Board, and are members of their national Association. There is, however, another quite separate code of flat green bowls played in eastern parts of England, where 741 clubs in 13 counties belong to the English Bowling Federation.

The EBF are not breakaway rivals of the EBA. They are an old established organisation, whose beginnings go back to the days before rink play had been invented and 'roving jack' was the normal game. As the term suggests, there were no territorial limits to a game, which could meander freely over a green in the same way that crown green games do today.

Federation bowlers are highly skilled at drawing to the jack, for, although today most EBF games are played in rinks, they keep the traditions of discouraging firing and disqualify bowls from counting as shots if they are more than six feet (1.83m) from the jack. No advantage is given to the toucher, and every bowl entering the ditch is declared dead.

Basically a two-wood game, most EBF championships are for two-wood singles, two-wood pairs, and two-wood rinks – a Federation rink meaning three players (fours is not a recognised EBF game). Moves have been made to introduce four-wood competitions, but the emphasis on two-wood bowling certainly puts a premium on drawing, as competitors in the Midland Bank World Pairs have found in the Association game's championship.

Mixed bowling is regarded favourably in the Federation, and there is a warm family feeling to their annual national championships which take place amongst fun and candy floss every August at Skegness.

Many bowlers play both EBF and EBA codes, sometimes at the same club and on the same green, and several of Engalnd's top drawing exponents learnt their exacting trade at the Federation game. John Ottaway, John Rednall, Roy Cutts, Bill Hobart and the Ward brothers, David and Chris are just a few of them.

The Federation has a lot to be proud of, not least that it makes the game of bowls accessible to many in country districts on what Association players would regard as inferior greens. It has an honoured place on the bowls scene today.

EBF championships are held in August every year at the Sun Castle Greens in Skegness.

GLOSSARY

Across Term used in crown green bowls to denote a tie, i.e., '5 across' means 5-all.

Across the head Description of a shot played narrow of the head, e.g., to take a bowl out of the count.

Arc The curve taken by the bowl, responding to the built-in bias.

Athletic stance The natural position of the body before delivery – basically a standing-up stance.

Attacking bowl A bowl delivered with more than enough weight to reach the target – perhaps with the intention of inflicting some damage.

Baby jack A jack delivered to the minimum length: 70 or 75 feet, according to which rules you are playing to.

Backhand Action of delivering a bowl on the left side of the rink – if you are right handed.

Back bowl/Back wood A bowl which finishes in a position behind the jack – often of value if the jack moves.

Back toucher A bowl that comes to rest touching the jack, and immediately behind it.

Backswing The early part of the delivery during which the arm moves backwards – preferably in a straight line.

Badges Cloth (sometimes wire) badges are worn on the blazer pocket to denote to which club, county or country the wearer belongs.

Banks The raised perimeter of the green, beyond the ditch.

Bias The lateral force which makes the bowl run in a curving path – caused by the eccentric shape of the bowl itself.

Be up to the head An expression often used by bowlers to suggest that nothing will change if your bowl finishes short of the head.

Blazer Worn proudly by every serious bowler to identify his club, county or country.

Blocker A bowl deliberately placed short of the jack to impede the opponent's access to the head.

Bocca A popular game played in Italy which is related to bowls.

Boules A popular game played in France which is related to bowls.

Bowl The mis-shapen spheroid, some 5 inches in diameter and 3½ pounds in weight that is the basic projectile in the game of bowls. Now made of high density plastic, but once made of Lignum Vitae (see WOODS).

Bowls bag A basic piece of equipment in which bowls, shoes, and other bowling paraphernalia are carried.

Bowling shoes At present, in Britain, shoes have to be brown in colour, with no hint of a heel, which might damage the bowling surface.

Bucketful A large score – maybe 6, 7 or 8 shots on one end of a team game, or 3 or 4 shots on one end of a game of singles.

Bundle Another term for a bucketful.

Callipers Measuring device employed when there is a relatively short distance between the wood and the jack.

Cannon A deflection obtained by a bowl during its original course on the green – often played for, but sometimes fortuitous. Also known as a WICK.

Carpet The synthetic substitute for turf used invariably indoors, and increasingly outdoors. Carpets may be of jute, felt, or man-made fibre.

Centre line The centre line of the rink is marked at its extremities by two white pegs on the bank at each end of the green. In the southern hemisphere, the line is marked in chalk to aid placement of mat and jack.

Chalk Another vital piece of equipment. Chalk is used to mark 'touchers', so that they may still count even if they fall into the ditch.

Claw The style of grip in which, with the thumb held high, the hand resembles a bird's foot.

Club The lifeblood of bowls is the club structure, which, in England, for example, binds nearly 2,700 clubs, in 36 counties, into a national association.

Concentration Perhaps the most vital factor ensuring success in competitive bowls.

Confidence Another vital factor in bowls as in all games.

Cot An alternative term for the JACK – used commonly in parts of East Anglia.

Count The number of shots scored on any one end – the term is used commonly to describe an unusually good harvest!

Cradle The style of grip where the bowl is 'cradled', or 'cupped' in the hand with little in the way of support or security.

Crouch The type of stance where knees and back are bent before secondary movement begins.

Crown green bowls The game of bowls as played in parts of the north of England and North Wales, where the centre area of the terrain is raised, and the green resembles an upturned saucer.

Dead bowl Any bowl which finishes outside the rink of play shall be accounted a dead bowl, and shall be removed to the bank for the remainder of the end. The exception, of course, is the toucher in the ditch, which is entitled to remain alive.

Dead end If the jack is driven beyond the bounds of the rink, the end shall be declared dead, and shall be replayed. A jack in the ditch is regarded as live as long as it is between the linear boundaries of the rink.

Dead length A bowl which is delivered precisely to the required distance is said to be a dead length bowl.

Disc Coloured discs, made of self-adhesive plastic, are often used these days to identify the teams of the bowls in play. The big disc is normally placed on the non-bias side of the bowl.

Ditch The green is bounded on four sides by a shallow ditch, into which the jack may be played, but in which bowls are accounted dead – unless they have touched the jack during their original course on the green, and have received the chalk mark due to all touchers.

Ditcher A bowl which enters the ditch.

Draw The basic shot in the game – delivered with only enough weight to travel the required distance. Also a term which refers to the amount of bend on a particular side of the rink, as in the expression, 'It's a big draw on that swinging hand'.

Drive – driving-shot (See also FIRE.) The act of putting considerable weight behind a delivery with the intention of hitting a target (a bowl or the jack) at speed, thereby changing an adverse head to one's favour.

Duster A useful piece of equipment, with which one may dry one's woods or one's hands when it is raining, or when the grass is wet.

Edge A fine contact between two bowls – or between bowl and jack.

End When all the bowls have been played in one direction an end has been completed. Only then may the shots be awarded, with any disputed shots being measured if necessary.

Fast green A surface which offers little in the way of friction to slow down the bowl, and which, therefore, needs very little effort to

reach the jack.

Feather A very fine contact on a stationary bowl which has hardly any effect on the direction of travel of the bowl in motion.

Federation bowls A variant of the flat green game, with its own set of rules and traditions – played in thirteen counties in the eastern part of England.

Fire – firing-shot (See also DRIVE.) The act of delivering a bowl at speed with a view to destroying your opponent's handiwork – maybe hitting his shots out of the count, or ditching the jack.

Firm wood A bowl delivered with some force, but not necessarily at top speed as in a firing-shot.

Fixed stance The type of body position adopted by a bowler seeking to eliminate all movement from his delivery, save that of his hand and arm.

Follow-through The extended movement of hand and arm, and body as well if appropriate, after the bowl has left the hand.

Footfault One foot has to be entirely within the confines of the mat for a delivery to be acceptable – and legal.

Forehand Action of delivering the bowl on the right side of the rink – if you are a right-handed bowler!

Fours Team play, where four players from one team are opposed by four from another, playing two bowls each, as lead, second, third and skip.

Front Toucher A wood that comes to rest touching the jack – and immediately in front of it, masking it from the view of the bowler on the mat.

Full-length jack The longest jack that can be played in flat green bowls is with the mat 2 yards from one ditch and the jack 2 yards from the other. On a 40 yard green, the playing distance would thus be 36 yards (32.9m).

Glide A fine contact on a stationary bowl which only marginally alters the course of the bowl in travel.

Green The surface on which the game of bowls is played – whether it is grass or artificial material, indoors or out. Also the width of the arc taken to the jack (also known as grass, land, or draw).

Grip The method by which the bowl is held in the hand.

Grippo A wax used to facilitate grip on the bowl – especially useful in wet conditions.

Grips The 'dimples' on some makes of bowls, placed there during manufacture, to assist the bowler in gripping the bowl.

Guard Another term for BLOCKER.

Head The collection of bowls around the jack at any one time, regardless of how far they are away from the target ball. Hence: a close head – when they are all near; and a scattered head – when they are not so near.

Heavy Bowl A bowl delivered with too much weight, which therefore travels too far.

Heavy Green A surface which offers much in the way of friction to slow down the moving bowl – and one which therefore requires some degree of physical strength to reach the jack when bowling a wood.

Heavyweight bowl A composition bowl made of a denser than standard material, and which is therefore heavier than the standard weight bowl.

Henselite The commercial name for the composition used in the manufacture of bowls by the Hensell family in Melbourne, Australia.

Indoor bowls Brought in as a winter substitute for the outdoor game, indoor bowls has blossomed and is now thriving in Britain.

International series The Home International Series, both outdoors and in, is the highlight of the season for bowlers in Britain.

Jack The little white ball close to which every bowler seeks to play his woods. Recently a yellow jack has been introduced for bowls on television. Also known as COT, KATE, KITTY, POT and WHITE.

Jack high Term denoting that a bowl or wood is level with the jack.

Jactu Lapidum Medieval game of stone throwing, thought to have given rise to the term for the target bowl – the jack.

Kate or kitty Another term for the JACK.

Killing the end Hitting the jack off the rink – either to the side, beyond the boundary strings, or over the bank beyond the ditch – makes a DEAD END.

'Last wood' Usually not the final wood of an end, but the spoken phrase by which the player or the marker acknowledges the previous delivery to be the shot. Short for 'The last wood is the shot'.

Laws of the game Rules framed by the IBB (outdoors) and the WIBC (indoors) to govern play throughout the world.

Lead The player in a team (pair, triple or four) who plays his bowls first.

Length Distance of the jack from the mat, and the concept of adjusting the strength of delivery to send the bowl the correct distance.

Lie The way the bowls are positioned around the jack. Specifically, a shot-lie, set-lie, match-lie or championship-lie suggests that a player holds sufficient shots to win as appropriate.

Lignum vitae The heaviest (most dense) wood in the world, from which all woods used to be made, before they invented high density plastic.

Line The direction in which the bowl has to be dispatched if it is to arc its path back to the jack. Hence, the concept of identifying that direction and achieving it in practice.

Line bowl A bowl so near the string that its status is debatable. Is it wholly beyond the confines of the rink? If so, it is a DEAD BOWL. If not, it is a LIVE BOWL.

Live bowl A bowl which comes to rest within the confines of the rink – this definition would include a TOUCHER in the ditch between the strings.

Luck A fickle lady, and a vital element in bowls.

Marker Official serving the players in a singles match, centring the jack, keeping the scorecard and giving information when requested.

Marks Some bowlers use marks – distant landmarks or irregular marks on the green itself – to help them find the correct line.

Master bowl The world standard bowl, of minimum bias, against which all sets of woods must be measured before they are stamped by the manufacturer.

Mat The mat marks the position from where all bowls will be delivered on a given end. One foot must be totally 'within the confines of the mat' at the moment of delivery or footfaulting occurs.

Mat-up-the-green A common tactic to unsettle the opponent is to take the mat some yards up the green. It must still be laid on the centre line, and there must be enough forward space for a minimum length jack (see BABY JACK).

Measure Who lies shot is guesswork until the last wood of an end is bowled and the measure is applied – where necessary. String, tape, callipers, feeler gauges and sonic devices can serve the purpose.

Mitchell Another occasional term for a TOUCHER – especially in Scotland. W. W. Mitchell was the Scot who first framed the Laws of the Game in 1849.

Narrow Description of a bowl delivered with insufficient green, therefore finishing across the head.

Neat weight Sufficient weight to do the job, but no more.

No end Another term for a DEAD END.

Pace Sometimes called the speed of the green, the pace determines how much weight you have to put behind your bowl so that it will reach the jack.

Pairs Team game for teams of two.

Petanque A popular game in France which is related to bowls.

Plant Two bowls lying in close proximity offer a plant. It is possible to predict with accuracy what will happen to bowl A when bowl B is struck.

Policeman or Bobby Another term for a BLOCKER.

Positional bowl A bowl placed deliberately away from the jack, for tactical reasons.

Possession of the rink A player is allowed freedom of the rink from the moment his opponent's wood comes to rest until his own next bowl comes to rest. At all other times, he should be behind either mat or head, standing discreetly to one side of the rink.

Pot Another regional variation for the JACK.

Push and lie A popular shot in Britain, where, with a firm wood, an opponent's bowl is hit out of the head, only to be replaced by the bowl in action.

Quick green Another term for FAST GREEN.

Reaching bowl A bowl delivered with more than drawing weight.

Replayed end A second attempt to play an end is necessary if it is killed at the first attempt. An end may also be replayed as a result of the Umpire's decision in the event of certain defaults.

Rest or Wrest A term describing how the opponent's shot may be beaten — by using it as a 'rest' or by 'wresting' it and settling in its place.

Rink The strip of green on which a game takes place — the width determined by the position of the boundary pegs, and marked out, sometimes, with string. Occasionally used as a term for four players who form a team.

Round-the-clock The unusual practice of playing backhand both ways, or forehand both ways, clockwise or anti-clockwise, as it were.

Rub-of-the-green The arbitrary intervention of luck has been expressed by this term since Shakespeare's day, if not before.

Run A trick in the playing surface which carries the bowl along a certain track, seemingly in spite of the action of the bias.

Runner A bowl delivered with weight, which misses its target and passes through the head, perhaps into the ditch.

Second The player in a four who plays his team's third and fourth bowls — and keeps the score.

Second bowl or Second wood The bowl or wood which has secured second position in the head — a very important defensive role.

Semi-crouch A mid-way stance between the upright athletic and the full crouch.

Set Another term for a PLANT.

Sets The game, fairly recently introduced, but growing in popularity, especially on television, where, instead of the traditional 21-up singles game, the result depends on who wins a given number of 7-up 'sets'.

Short bowl A bowl delivered with insufficient weight to reach its desired destination. Often much criticised by experts on the bank — who were knocked out in the previous round!

Short jack A jack length preferred by many touch players — but the jack must be at least 70 (sometimes 75) feet (21.3 or 22.9m) from the delivery mat.

Short mat An indoor variant of the game of bowls, introduced in the 1930's in Ireland and South Wales, in Workingmen's Clubs and Church Halls, as a winter pastime, and now a flourishing game in its own right.

Shot or Shot bowl The shot bowl is the one nearest to the jack. Shots are scored according to the number of bowls you have nearer to the jack than your opponent's nearest.

Shoulder The point on the arc, curve or swing of the bowl where it seems to break back most markedly — the widest point of the draw. The term is also used to describe a bowl short of the head which could be used to gain access.

Singles The head-to-head game between two players, each bowling four woods, traditionally played to 21-up, but at international level recently changed to 25-up, and sometimes played to the sets format.

Skip The player who bowls last and captains the team in a pairs, triples or fours game.

Split An inviting target of two bowls, side by side, with a narrow gap in between them. A running bowl can remove both of them, and remain in the area for shot — the perfect split.

Springing the jack The action of moving the jack — sometimes some considerable distance — by tapping the bowl that is touching it.

Sonic measure Measuring device utilising sonic beams and displaying the distances digitally. Not yet fully accepted by all players, but has received the approval of many top officials.

South African clinic A style of delivery developed in South Africa by Dr Julius Serge.

Stance The initial posture on the mat, before the process of delivery begins.

Straight hand or Straight side Hardly ever literally 'straight', one side of the rink often swings less than the other. This is called the straight hand.

String The thread which marks the boundary of the rink. Hence expressions such as 'Out to the string' or 'Over the string'. A bowl may pass over the string during its travel, as long as it returns to the rink of play at the end of its run.

Surbowl A commercially produced gripping agent to facilitate grip in wet conditions.

Swing The common term for the curve or arc of the bowl as it responds to the influence of the bias.

Take-out The act of pushing an opponent's shot or saving bowl out of the head, to make the shot or shots for oneself.

Target bowls A variant of flat green bowls, where the jack is replaced by a target mat marked in a similar fashion to an archery target. Introduced in the 1970s, the idea never really took off in a big way.

Third man The player who delivers his team's fifth and sixth woods in a game of fours, and is normally called upon to measure disputed shots.

Thomas Taylor The oldest manufacturer of bowls in Britain, still run, like Hensell's operation in Australia, by members of the original family – Noel Taylor is the current Director.

Tied end When, after a measure for shot, it is agreed that the two bowls in contention can not be separated – they are equidistant from the jack – no score is awarded, but the end is regarded as having been played, i.e. it does not have to be replayed.

Tight Another expression meaning NARROW. Not enough GREEN has been given to the bowl.

Tight head A head with lots of bowls surrounding the jack.

Timing a green The pace of a green is measured in seconds – the time it takes for a bowl on an unobstructed course to come to rest 30 yards away from where it was delivered can be timed with a stop-watch.

Timing-shot The bowl is delivered with less than firing weight, so that it still bends with the bias. Scottish bowlers use the expression a lot, and say they are giving the bowl 'time to bend'.

Toucher A bowl that touches the jack during its original course on the green is deemed a 'toucher', and is marked with chalk. This chalk-mark will help to identify it if it finds its way into the ditch at any stage during the end, when, unlike non-touchers, it will remain a live bowl.

Tossing a coin The toss of a coin determines who shall deliver the first jack. The winner of the toss may himself go first, or he may give the honour to his opponent.

Track/Tracking On soft outdoor greens in Britain, the rolling of the surface by a succession of bowls is inclined to leave the green tracked with grooves. These act rather like tram-lines, taking the rolling bowl where the impetus and the bias never intended it to go.

Trail A gently overweighted delivery can collect the jack and take it to a more secure or profitable location. This is called 'trailing the jack'.

Triples The team game consisting of three-a-side, where each player uses three bowls, and the game normally lasts 18 ends.

Umpire The official whose decision must be final. He is there to implement the Laws of the Game, but, like all good officials, he does so discreetly, and with due deference to the spirit behind the Laws.

Wall Sometimes a line of bowls develops, and effectively builds a wall. This may obstruct access to the head, or may offer possibilities to a clever player, who may be able to use the wall to bounce off – a trick called a wick, a ricochet, a feather or a glide.

Waterproofs A standard item of gear in the bowls bag of every British bowler. Should be white, of course.

Wedge Triangular piece of wood found in every Umpire's kit, and used for propping bowls to prevent movement during the course of measuring.

Weight The common term for impetus, momentum, length, or power.

White 'The white' is another name for the JACK – one of several interesting regional variations.

Wick The bowler's term for a ricochet – sometimes played for; sometimes, regrettably, not. Consequently, the word is not always used politely, and is often preceded by another, less polite word.

Wide If a bowl finishes wide of its desired position, it has been given too much green.

World Bowls The short name for the World outdoor championships which are played every four years. Those held in Auckland in 1988 were the Sixth World Bowls Championships. The Seventh will be played in Worthing in 1992, and the Eighth in Salisbury, South Australia in 1996.

Wrong bias The shot no-one wants to play – the bowl is delivered with the bias (the little disc) on the wrong side, and swings against expectations onto the next rink. Drinks all round!

Yard-on A much misused term which *should* mean playing with one yard more weight than you would if you were simply drawing. Often, used loosely, it means anything from one yard of weight to a full-blooded drive.

LAWS OF THE GAME

REPRODUCED BY KIND PERMISSION OF THE WORLD INDOORS BOWLS COUNCIL

The Laws of the outdoor game are revised from time to time by the International Bowling Board. These are printed in the annual EBA Handbook and are readily available. Here are the Laws of the indoor game, formulated by the World Indoor Bowls Council, which differ only in minor details, and which, given the growing interest in indoor bowls through television exposure, are probably of greater relevance to the average reader.

(1) It should be appreciated that no code of Laws governing a game has yet achieved such perfection as to cope with every situation. The code of Laws governing bowls is no exception. Unusual incidents not definitely provided for in the Laws frequently occur. It is well, therefore, to remember that the Laws have been framed in the belief that true sportsmanship will prevail, and that in the absence of any express rule common sense will find a way to complete a happy solution to a knotty problem.

(2) The World Indoor Bowls Council, wherever both desirable and practicable, have formulated these Laws in terms that they harmonise with the Laws of the Game of the International Bowling Board.

(3) Acknowledgement is also made to the English Indoor Bowling Association and the W.I.B.C. Laws of the Game Sub-Committee.
The members of the Sub-Committee were Mr James Barclay (Committee Secretary, Scotland); Mr William Burrows (Ireland); Mr Harry Death (England) and Mr Ronald Thomas (Wales).

(4) The World Indoor Bowls Council Laws of the Game governing Indoor Bowls will apply to all competitive play involving Ladies, Gents or mixed play. Any amendments to these Laws of the Game will require to be approved in advance of implementation by the W.I.B.C.

(5) It is the responsibility of all Players, Umpires and Markers to refrain at all times from committing any act which is liable in any way to cause damage to the Indoor Green or Carpet.

DEFINITIONS

1. (a) 'Controlling Body' means the body having immediate control of the conditions under which a match is played. The order shall be:
    (i) World Indoor Bowls Council.
    (ii) The Member Governing Body.
    (iii) The County Governing Body.
    (iv) The Club on whose Green the match is being played.
   (b) 'Skip' means the player who, for the time being, is in charge of the head on behalf of the team.
   (c) 'Team' means either a four, triple or a pair.
   (d) 'Side' means any agreed number of teams, whose combined scores determine the results of the match.
   (e) 'Four' means a team of four players whose positions in order of playing are named Lead, Second, Third, Skip.
   (f) 'Bowl in Course' means a bowl from the time of its delivery until it comes to rest.
   (g) 'End' means the playing of the Jack and all the bowls of all the opponents in the same direction on a rink.
   (h) 'Head' means the Jack and such bowls as have come to rest within the boundary of the rink and are not dead.
   (i) 'Mat-Line' means the edge of the mat which is nearest to the front ditch. From the centre of the Mat-Line all necessary measurements to the nearest point of Jack or bowls shall be taken.

   (j) 'Master Bowl' means a bowl which has been approved by the International Bowling Board and the World Indoor Bowls Council, as having the minumum bias required, as well as in all other respects complying with the laws of the Game governing both Indoor and Outdoor Bowls, and is engraved with the words 'Master Bowl'.
    (i) A 'Standard Bowl' meeting the same criteria as the 'Master Bowl' shall be kept in the custody of each Member Governing Body.
    (ii) A 'Standard Bowl' shall be provided for the use of each Official Licensed Bowls Tester.
   (k) 'Jack High' means that the nearest portion of the bowl referred to is in line with and at the same distance from the Mat-Line as the nearest portion of the Jack.
   (l) 'Pace of Green' means the number of seconds taken by a bowl from the time of delivery to the moment it comes to rest, approximately 90 feet (27.43 metres) from the Mat-Line.
   (m) 'Displaced' as applied to the Jack or bowl means 'disturbed' by any agency that is not sanctioned by these Laws.
   (n) 'Ditch Holding Surface' means some material other than the carpet to stop the Jack or bowl from running along the ditch.
   (o) 'Set'. A set is a pre-determined number of ends or shots forming part of the overall game.
   (p) A set of bowls means four bowls comprising a matched set which are the same size, weight, colour, bias, serial number and engraving where applicable. In all games each player shall play with the appropriate number of bowls from the same set of bowls.

THE INDOOR GREEN

2. **The Indoor Green**
3. **The Ditch**
4. **The banks**
All reference to Laws 2, 3 and 4 have been removed and are located at the end of this booklet in the Code of Practice.
5. **Division of Green**
The Indoor Green shall be divided into sections called rinks. Each rink shall be of a uniform length and width. Rinks used for competitions played under the direct control of the World Indoor Bowls Council shall not be less than 15 feet (4.57 metres) nor more than 19 feet (5.79 metres) in width. The rinks shall be numbered consecutively and the numbers may be placed on the face of the bank, on top of the bank, or on the wall behind the bank, but shall always be on the centre line of the rink. The centre of the rink shall be clearly indicated. The four corners of the rink shall be indicated by markers, affixed to the face of the bank and flush therewith, or alternately fixed on the bank not more than 4 inches (102 mm) back from the face thereof. These

markers shall be of a material which cannot cause damage to bowls or Jack. The marker shall be not more than 1 inch (25.4 mm) in width, and the centre of the marker shall be clearly marked by a thin black line. Similar markers shall be fixed to the side banks to indicate a clear distance of 81 feet (24.7 metres) from the end ditch on the line of play. An unobtrusive marker in the form of a 'T' may be affixed to the carpet with the short leg of the 'T' being parallel to and 6 feet (1.8 metres) from the edge of the ditch, the junction indicating the centre line of the rink. The World Indoors Bowls Council reserves the right to put additional marks/markers on the Indoor Green to assist with the positioning of the mat and/or centring the Jack. In the event of part of the Indoor Green being used to accomodate spectators, side ditches may be dispensed with, but the distance markers must be brought forward and fixed in a suitable manner. They must be clearly visible to all players. During the period of provision of temporary seating on the Indoor Green, there must be a completely unrestricted area of the Indoor Green, of at least 3 feet (91.5 cm) in width between the seated area and the outside boundary of the nearest rink.

6. Permissable Variations to Law 5
Variation to Law 5 will only be permitted by the appropriate Controlling Body if (a) it can be established to the satisfaction of the Controlling Body that such variation is essential to the efficient running of the club concerned, or (b) such variation is permitted under National Competition Rules.

7. Mat
The mat shall be of definite size, namely 24 inches (61 cm) long and 14 inches (35.6 cm) wide.

8. The Jack
The Jack shall be spherical and white in colour acceptable to the World Indoor Bowls Council, with a diameter of not less than 2 15/32 inches (62.70 mm) nor more than 2 21/32 inches (66.60 mm). It shall be not less that 13½ oz (382 gm) nor more than 16 oz (453 gm) in weight.

9. Bowls
(a) (i) Bowls shall be made of wood, rubber or composition and shall be black or brown in colour. The World Indoor Bowls Council, The British Isles Indoor Bowls Council and each of the Member Governing Bodies reserve the right to authorise play with bowls other than black or brown in colour.
Each bowl of a set shall bear the member's individual and distinguishing mark on each side. The provision relating to the distinguishing mark on each side of the bowl need not apply other than in competitions under the direct control of the W.I.B.C., or the B.I.I.B.C.. Bowls made of wood (lignum vitae) shall have a maximum diameter of 5¼ inches (133.35 mm) and a minimum diameter of 4⅝ inches (1.59 k/g). Loading of bowls is strictly prohibited.
(ii) In all bowls matches played under the direct control of the W.I.B.C., B.I.I.B.C. or Member Governing Bodies a bowl made of rubber or composition shall have a maximum diameter of 5⅛ inches (130.17 mm) and a minimum diameter of 4⅝ inches (117,5 mm), and the weight shall not exceed 3 lb 8 oz (1.59 k/g).
(iii) The Controlling Body may, at its discretion, supply and require players to affix temporarily an adhesive marking to their bowls in any competition game. Any temporary marking under this Law shall be regarded as part of the bowl for all purposes under these Laws.
(b) The Master Bowl shall have a bias approval by the I.B.B. and the W.I.B.C. A bowl shall have a bias not less than that of the Master Bowl, and shall bear the imprint of the stamp of the I.B.B. To ensure accuracy of bias and visibility of the stamp, all bowls shall be re-tested and re-stamped at least once every ten years or earlier, if the date of the stamp is not clearly legible.
The W.I.B.C., the B.I.I.B.C., and the Member Governing Bodies reserve the right to test any bowls intended for play in any Indoor Bowls event under their direct control. The test may

be a table test or a green test depending on the availability of test facilties.
(c) **Bowls failing Test.**
If a bowl in the hands of a Licensed Tester has been declared as not complying with 9(b), it shall be altered, if possible, to comply, before being returned. The owner of the bowl shall be responsible for the expense involved. If the bowl cannot be altered to comply with 9(a) and (b), any current official stamp appearing thereon shall be cancelled by the Tester by stamping an X over any current official stamp.
(d) **Objection to Bowls.**
A challenge may be lodged by an opposing player and/or by the Official Umpire and/or by the Controlling Body. A challenge or any intimation thereof shall not be lodged with any opposing player during the progress of a match. A challenge may be lodged with the Umpire at any time during a match, provided the Umpire is not a player in that or any other match of the same competition. If a challenge be lodged, it shall be made not later than ten minutes after the completion of the final end in which the bowl was used.
Once a challenge is lodged with the Umpire, it cannot be withdrawn.
The challenge shall be based on the grounds that the bowl does not comply with one or more or the requirements set out in Law 9(a) and 9(b).
The Umpire shall request the user of the bowl to surrender it to him for forwarding to the Controlling Body. If the owner of the challenged bowl refuses to surrender it to the Umpire, the match shall thereupon be forfeited to the opponent. The user or owner, or both, may be disqualified from playing in any match controlled or permitted by the Controlling Body, so long as the bowl remains untested by a Licensed Tester.
On receipt of the bowl, the Umpire shall take immediate steps to hand it to the Secretary of the Controlling body, who shall arrange for a table test to be made as soon as practicable, and in the presence of a representative of the Controlling Body.
If a table test be not readily available, and any delay would unduly interfere with the progress of the competition, then, should an aproved green testing device be available, it may be used to make an immediate test on the green. If a green test be made, it shall be done by, or in the presence of the Umpire over a distance of not less than 75 feet (22.8 metres). The comparison shall be between the challenged bowl and a standard bowl, or if it be not readily available, then a recently stamped bowl of similar size, or nearly so, should be used.
The decision of the Umpire, as a result of the test, shall be final and binding for that match. The result of the subsequent table test shall not invalidate the decision given by the Umpire on the green test.
If a challenged bowl, after an official table test, be found to comply with all the requirements of Law 9(a) and 9(b), it shall be returned to the user or owner.
If the challenged bowl be found not to comply with Law 9(a) and 9(b), the match it was played shall be forfeited to the opponent.
(e) **Alteration to bias.**
A player shall not alter, or cause to be altered other than by an Official Bowl Tester, the bias of any bowl bearing the imprint of the official stamp of the I.B.B., under penalty of suspension from playing for a period to be determined by the Member Governing Body to which his club is affiliated. Such suspension shall be subject to confirmation by the B.I.I.B.C and the W.I.B.C. If the suspension is agreed then the ban will be operative in all countries in membership of the Governing Bodies who approve the ban.

10. Footwear
Players, Umpires and Markers shall wear black, brown or white smooth soled heel-less shoes while playing, acting as an Umpire or Marker on an Indoor Green.
N.B. Shoe under circumstances of disability may

also include boot.

ARRANGING A GAME
11. General Form and Duration
A game of bowls shall be played on one rink or on several rinks. It shall consist of a specific number of shots or ends, or shall be played for any period of time as previously arranged. The Ends of the game shall be played alternatively in opposite directions excepting as provided in Laws 38, 42, 44, 46 and 47.

12. Selecting the Rinks for Play – Umpire to Witness
When a match is to played, the draw for the rinks to be played on shall be made by the skips or their representatives in the presence of the Umpire. The actual rinks used will be decided by the club at which the game or games are played. In a match for a trophy or where competing skips have been drawn previously, the draw to decide the number of the rinks to be played on shall be made by the visiting skips or their representatives again in the presence of the Umpire. No player in a competition or match shall play or practise on the same rink on the day of such competition or match before play commences under penalty of disqualification. This Law shall not apply in the case of Open Tournaments. For all National Association Competitions see the appropriate Competition Rules.

13. Play Arrangements
Games shall be organised in the following play arrangements:
   (a) As a single game.
   (b) As a team game
   (c) As a sides game.
   (d) As a series of single games, team games or side games.
   (e) As a special tournament of games.

14. A single game shall be played on one rink of a green as a single handed game by two contending players, each playing two, three or four bowls singly and alternately.
15. A pairs game shall be played by two contending teams of two players called lead and skip according to the order in which they play. Each player playing two, three or four bowls singly and alternately. The number of bowls being previously arranged by the Controlling Body.
16. A triples game shall be played by two contending teams of three players who shall play two or three bowls singly and alternately. The leads shall play first. The number of bowls previously arranged by the Controlling Body.
17. A fours game shall be played by two contending teams of four players, each player playing two bowls singly and alternately.
18. A side game shall be played by two contending sides each composed of an equal number of teams.
19. Games in series shall be arranged to be played on several and consecutive occasions as:
(a) a series or sequence of games, organised in the form of an eliminating competition, and arranged as singles, pairs, triples or fours.
(b) a series or sequence of side matches organised in the form of a league competition, or an eliminating competition, or of inter-association matches.

20. A Special Tournament of Games
Single games and team games may also be arranged in group form as a special tournament of games in which the contestants play each other in turn, or they may play as paired-off teams of players on one or several greens in accordance with a common time-table, success being adjudged by the number of games won, or by the highest net score in shots in accordance with the regulations governing the tournament.

21 For Championships and International Matches where played:
In all forms of competitive play under the direct control of the World Indoor Bowls Council each player shall play the same number of bowls as his direct opponent. In competitive indoor bowls play there will normally be a time limit on play. The

time restriction on play will be determined by the Controlling Body in advance of the commencement of play, and time limits must always be taken into consideration with the following sub-paragraphs (i) (ii) (iv) (v)

(i)   Singles may be played with two, three or four bowls each player playing alternately. Singles shall be of twenty-one (21) shots or such other format as agreed in advance by the Controlling Body. (Shots in excess of the pre-determined total shall not count.)

(ii) Pairs shall be of twenty-one (21) ends, and may be played with two, three or four bowls, each player playing alternately.

(iii) Triples shall be of eighteen (18) ends, and may be played with two or three bowls, each player playing alternately.

(iv) Fours shall be of twenty-one (21) ends, two bowls each player and played alternately.

(v)   Side games under the direct control of the World Indoor Bowls Council shall be of twenty-one (21) ends, provided that pairs, triples and fours may be of a lesser number of ends, but in the case of pairs and fours there shall be not less than eighteen (18) ends, and in the case of triples not less than fifteen (15) ends, subject in all cases to the express approval of the World Indoor Bowls Council as represented by its senior officer present. If no such officer be present at the time then the decision shall rest with the Controlling Body as defined in Law 1. Any decision to curtail the number of ends to be played shall be made before the commencement of any game and such decision shall only be due to, or on the grounds of, shortage of time to complete a programme. In the event of a power failure causing a 'Blackout' the Controlling Body shall determine what course of action to be taken.

22. Awards
Cancelled; see By-laws after Law 73 under heading 'Players' Status'.

STARTING THE GAME
23.
(a) Trial Ends
Before start of play in any competition, match or game, or on the resumption of an unfinished competition, match or game on another day, not more than one trial end each way shall be played.
(b) Tossing for opening play
The captains in a side game, skips in a team game, or opponents in a singles game shall toss to decide which side, team or opponent shall play first. The winner of the toss has the option of decision. In the event of a tied (no score) or a 'dead' end, the first to play in the tied or 'dead' end shall again play first. In all ends subsequent to the first end, the winner of the preceding scoring end shall play first.
24. Placing the Mat
At the beginning of the first end the player to play first shall place the centre line of the mat lengthwise on the centre line of the rink, the front edge of the mat to be 6 feet (1.84 metres) from the ditch.
25. The Mat and its Replacement
After play has commenced in any end, the mat shall not be moved from its first position except in the following circumstances:-
(a) If the mat be displaced during the progress of the end, it shall be replaced as near as practicable in the same position.
(b) If the mat be out of alignment with the centre line of the rink, it may be straightened at any time during the end.
(c) After the last bowl in each end has come to rest in play, or has sooner become 'dead', the mat shall be lifted and placed beyond the face of the rear bank.
     Should the mat be picked up by a player before the end as been completed, the opposing player shall have the right of replacing the mat in its original position.
26. The Mat and Jack in subsequent Ends.
(a) In all subsequent ends the front edge of the mat shall be not less than 6 feet (1.84 metres) from the rear ditch, and not less than 81 feet (24.7 metres) from the front ditch and on the centre line of the rink of play.

(b) Should the Jack be improperly delivered under Law 30 the opposing player may move the mat in the line of play, subject to Clause (a) above, and deliver the Jack, but shall not play first. Should the Jack be improperly delivered twice by each player in any end, it shall not be delivered again in that end, but shall be centred with the nearest portion of the Jack to the mat line being 6 feet (1.84 metres) from the edge of the front ditch, and the mat placed at the option of the first to play.
If after the Jack is set as described in this Clause, the end is made 'dead' the winner of the previous scoring end shall deliver the Jack, when the end is played anew.
(c) No one shall be permitted to challenge the legality of the original position of the mat after the first to play has delivered the first bowl.
27. Stance on Mat
A player shall take his stance on the mat, and at the moment of delivering the Jack or his bowl, shall have one foot remaining entirely within the confines of the mat. The foot may be either in contact with, or over the mat. Failure to observe this Law constitutes foot-faulting.
28. Foot-faulting
Should a player infringe the Law of foot-faulting, the Umpire may, after having given a warning, have the bowl stopped and declared 'dead'. If the bowl has disturbed the head, the opponents shall have the option of either:-
(i)   Resetting the Head,
(ii) Leaving the head as altered
       Or
(iii) Declaring the end 'dead'.
29. Delivering the Jack
The player to play first shall deliver the Jack. If the Jack in its original course comes to rest at a distance of less than 6 feet (1.84 metres) from the edge of the front ditch, it shall be moved out and centred with the nearest portion of the Jack to the mat line being 6 feet (1.84 metres) from the edge of the front ditch. If the Jack during its original course is obstructed or deflected by a neutral object, neutral person, marker, opponent or member of the opposing team, it shall be re-delivered by the same player. Should the obstruction or deflection be caused by a member of his own team, the Jack shall be delivered by the lead of the opposing team. Under these circumstances the opposing lead is entitled to reset the mat.
30. Jack improperly delivered
If the Jack in the first or any subsequent end is not delivered from a proper stance on the mat, which has been properly located on the centre line of the rink, or if it ends its original course in the ditch, or totally outside the side boundaries of the rink, or it is less than 75 feet (22.8 metres) measured in a straight line from the centre of the front edge of the mat to the nearest point of the Jack, after the Jack has been located on the centre line of the rink, it shall be returned and the opposing player shall deliver the Jack, but shall not play first. The Jack shall be returned if it is improperly delivered, but the right of the player first delivering the Jack in that end to play first shall not be affected, see (Law 26b).No one shall be permitted to challenge the legality of the original length of the Jack after the first to play has delivered the first bowl.
31. Variation to Laws
Any Member Governing Body may, with the prior approval of the World Indoor Bowls Council, vary any of the distances mentioned in these Laws of the Game governing Indoor Bowls.

MOVEMENT OF BOWLS
32. 'Live' Bowl
A bowl which in its original course on the indoor green comes to rest with any part of the bowl being within the boundaries of the rink, and not being less than 45 feet (13.71 metres) from the centre of the front edge of the mat to the nearest point of the bowl, shall be accounted to be a 'Live' bowl and shall be in play.
33. 'Touchers'
A bowl which on its original course on the green touches the Jack even though such bowl passes into the ditch within the boundaries of the rink shall be a 'live' bowl and shall be called a

'toucher'. If after having come to rest a bowl falls over and touches the Jack BEFORE THE NEXT BOWL IS DELIVERED, or in the case of the last bowl of an end it falls and touches the Jack within th period of half a minute invoked under Law 53, such bowl shall also be a 'toucher'. No bowl shall be accounted a 'toucher' by playing on to, or by coming in contact with the Jack while the Jack is in the ditch.
If a 'toucher' in the ditch cannot be seen from the mat, its position shall be marked by a coloured marker about 2 inches (51 mm) broad and not more than 4 inches (102 mm) in height placed on top of, or on the face of the bank, and immediately in line with the place where the 'toucher' rests.
34. Marking a 'Toucher'
A 'toucher' shall be clearly marked with a chalk mark by a member of the player's team. If in the opinion of either skip or opponents in singles play a 'toucher' or wrongly marked bowl comes to rest in such a position that the act of marking or erasing such a mark is likely to move the bowl or to alter the head, the bowl shall not be marked or have its mark erased but shall be 'indicated' as a 'toucher' or 'non toucher' as the case may be. If a bowl is not so marked or not so 'indicated' BEFORE THE SUCCEEDING BOWL COMES TO REST it ceases to be a 'toucher'. If both skips or opponents agree than any subsequent movement of the bowl eliminates the necessity for continuation of the 'indicated' provision, the bowl shall thereupon be marked or have the mark erased as the case may be. Care should be taken to remove 'toucher' marks from all bowls before they are played, but should a player fail to do so, and should the bowl not become a 'toucher' in the end in play, the mark shall be removed by the opposing skip, his deputy or the marker, immediately the bowl comes to rest, unless the bowl is 'indicated' as a 'non-toucher' in circumstances governed by earlier provisions of this Law.
35. Movements of 'touchers'
A 'toucher' in play in the ditch may be moved by the impact of a Jack in play or of another 'toucher' in play, and also by the impact of a 'non-toucher' which remains in play after the impact, and any movements of the 'toucher' by such incidents shall be valid. However, should the 'non-toucher' enter the ditch at any time after the impact, it shall be 'dead', and the 'toucher' shall be deemed to have been displaced by a 'dead' bowl and the provisions of Law 38(d) shall apply.
36. Bowl accounted 'Dead'
(a) Without limiting the application of any other of these Laws a bowl shall be accounted 'dead' if it:
     (i)   being a 'non-toucher' comes to rest in the ditch, or rebounds on to the playing surface of the rink, after contact with the bank or side wall, or with a Jack or a 'toucher' in the ditch or
     (ii) after completing its original course, or after being moved as a result of play, it comes to rest wholly outside the boundaries of the playing surface of the rink, or if when measured in a straight line from the centre of the front edge of the mat to the nearest point of the bowl, this distance is less than 45 feet (13.71 metres) or
     (iii) in its original course passes beyond a side boundary of the rink on a bias which would prevent it re-entering the rink.
(b) Skips or opponents in singles shall agree on the question as to whether or not a bowl is 'dead'. Any member of either team may request a decision from the skips, but no member shall remove any bowl prior to agreement by the skips. Once their attention has been drawn to the matter, the skips by agreement must make a decision. If they cannot reach agreement, the Umpire must make an immediate decision.
36. Bowl Rebounding
Only 'touchers' rebounding from the face of the bank to the ditch or to the rink shall remain in play
38. Bowl displacement
(a) Displacement by rebounding 'non toucher':-

A bowl displaced by 'non toucher' rebounding from the bank shall be restored as near as possible to its original position, by a member of the opposing team.

(b) Displacement by a participating player:-
If a bowl while in motion or at rest on the green, or a 'toucher' in the ditch, is interfered with or displaced by one of the players, the opposing skip shall have the option of:-
(i) restoring the bowl as near as possible to its original position
(ii) letting the bowl remain where it rests
(iii) declaring the end 'dead'
(v) declaring the end 'dead'.

(c) (i) Displacement by a neutral object or neutral person, of a bowl in its original course (other than as provided in clause (d) hereof). If such bowl be displaced within the boundaries of the rink of play without having disturbed the head, it shall be replayed. If it be displaced and it has disturbed the heads the skips or opponents in singles shall reach agreement on the final position of the displaced bowl, and on the replacement of the head, otherwise the end shall be 'dead'. These provisions shall also apply to a bowl in its original course which is displaced outside the boundaries of the rink of play, provided such bowl was running on a bias which would have enabled it to re-enter the rink.
(ii) Displacement of a bowl at rest, or in motion as a result of play after being at rest:-
If such bowl be displaced, the skips or opponents in singles, shall come to an agreement as to the position of the bowl and of the replacement of any part of the head disturbed by the displaced bowl, otherwise the end shall be 'dead'.

(d) Displacement of a 'toucher' in the ditch by a 'dead' bowl from the rink of play:-
it shall be restored as near as possible to its original position by a player of the opposite team, or by the marker.

(e) If a bowl in motion and on its original course collides with a similar bowl from another rink, the bowls shall be returned to the respective players for re-delivery

(f) Displacement inadvertently produced:
If a bowl be moved at the time of its being marked or measured it shall be restored as near as possible to its original position by an opponent. If the displacement is caused by a marker or umpire, then the marker or umpire shall replace the bowl.

39. 'Line Bowls'
A bowl shall not be accounted as outside any line unless it be entirely clear of it. This shall be ascertained by looking perpendicularly down on the bowl or by placing a square on the green, or by the use of a string or mirror or other optical device.

MOVEMENT OF JACK
40. A 'live' Jack in the Ditch
A Jack moved by a bowl in play into the front ditch within the boundaries of the rink shall be deemed to be 'live'. It may be moved by the impact of a 'toucher' in play and also by the impact of a 'non-toucher' which remains in play after the impact; any movement of the Jack by such incidents shall be valid. However, should the 'non-toucher' enter the ditch after impact, it shall be 'dead' and the Jack shall be deemed to have been 'displaced' by a 'dead' bowl and the provisions of Law 48 shall apply. If the Jack in the ditch cannot be seen from the mat its position shall be marked by a marker about 2 inches (51 mm) in height, placed on top of, or on the face of, the bank and immediately in line from the place where the Jack rests.

41. A Jack accounted 'Dead'
Should the Jack be driven by a bowl in play and come to rest wholly beyond the boundary of the rink, i.e. over the bank, or over the side boundary, or into any opening or inequality of any kind in the bank, or rebound to a distance of less than 66 feet (20.1 metres) in direct line from the centre of the front edge of the mat to the nearest point of the Jack in its rebounded position, it shall be accounted 'dead'.

42. 'Dead' End
When the jack is 'dead' the end shall be regarded as a 'dead' end and shall not be accounted as a played end even though all the bowls in that end have been played. All 'dead' ends shall be played anew in the same direction unless both skips or opponents in singles agree to play in the opposite direction.
After a 'dead' end situation the right to deliver the Jack shall always return to the player who delivered the original Jack.

43. Playing to a boundary Jack
The Jack, if driven to the side boundary of the rink and not wholly beyond its limits; may be played to on either hand, and if necessary, a bowl may pass outside the side limits of the rink. A bowl so played, which comes to rest within the boundaries of the rink, shall not be accounted 'dead'. If the Jack be driven to the side boundary line and come to rest partly within the limits of the rink and coming to rest entirely outside the boundary line, even though it has made contact with the Jack, shall be accounted "dead" and shall be removed to the bank by a member of the player's team.

44. A Damaged Jack
In the event of the Jack being damaged, the Umpire shall decide if another Jack is necessary and, if so, the end shall be regarded as a 'dead' end and another Jack shall be substituted and the end shall be replayed anew.

45. A Rebounding Jack
If the Jack be driven against the face of the bank and rebound on to the rink, or after being played into the ditch, it be operated on by a 'toucher' so as to find its way on to the rink, it shall be played to in the same manner as if it had never left the rink.

46. Jack displaced by a player
(a) If the Jack be diverted from its course while in motion on the green, or displaced while at rest on the green, or in the ditch, by any one of the players, the opposing skip shall have the option of:
(i) restoring the Jack as near as possible to its original position,
(ii) letting the Jack remain where it rests, and play the end to a finish,
or
(iii) declaring the end 'dead'.

(b) Displacement inadvertently produced:
If a Jack be moved at the time of measuring, it shall be restored as near as possible to its original position by an opponent.

47. Jack displaced by a non-player
(a) If the Jack whether in motion or at rest on the rink, or in the ditch, be displaced by an individual not a member of the team, or by a bowl from another rink, or by any object, the two skips or the opponents in a singles game shall decide as to the original position of the Jack. If they are unable to agree the end in question shall be declared 'dead'.

(b) If the Jack be displaced by a Marker or Umpire, in the process of measuring or in any other circumstances, the displaced Jack shall be restored as near as possible to its original position by the Marker or Umpire, of which he shall be the sole Judge.

48. Jack displaced by 'non-toucher'
A Jack displaced in the rink of play by a 'non-toucher' rebounding from the bank shall be restored as near as possible to its original position, by a player of the opposing team. Should a Jack however after having been played into the ditch, be displaced by a 'dead' bowl, it shall be restored as near as possible to its original position by a player of the opposing team or by the marker.

FOURS PLAY
The basis of the Game of Bowls is Fours Play

49. Fours Play
(a) Designation of players. A team shall consist of four players, named respectively lead, second, third and skip, according to the order in which they play. Each player shall play two bowls.

(b) Order of Play. The leads shall play their two bowls alternately, and so on, each pair of players in succession to the conclusion of the end. No one shall play until his opponent's bowl has come to rest.

Except under the circumstances provided for in Law 63, the order of play shall not be changed after the first end has been played, under penalty of disqualification, with the match being forfeited to the opposing team.

50. Possession of the Rink
Possession of the rink shall belong to the team whose bowl is being played. The players in possession of the rink for the time being shall not be interfered with, annoyed, or have their attention distracted in any way by their opponents. As soon as each bowl shall have come to rest, possession of the rink shall be transferred to the other team, time being allowed for marking a 'toucher'.

51. Position of Players
Players of each team not in the act of playing or controlling play shall stand behind the Jack and away from the head, or 3 feet (92 cm) behind the mat. As soon as the bowl is delivered, the skip or player directing the head, if in front of the Jack shall retire behind it. In cases where there is no 'stand-off' room at the end of the rink, players shall stand well clear off the object bowl or Jack while a bowl is being delivered.

52. Players and their duties
(a) The skip shall have sole charge of his team, and his instructions shall be observed by his players. With the opposing skip he shall decide all disputed points, and when both agree their decision shall be final. If both skips cannot agree, the point in dispute shall be referred to, and considered by, an Umpire whose decision shall be final.
A skip may at any time delegate his powers and any of his duties to other members of his team provided that such delegation is notified to the opposing skip.

(b) The third player may have delegated to him the duty of measuring any and all disputed shots.

(c) The second player shall keep a record of all shots scored for and against his team, and shall at all times retain possession of the score card whilst play is in progress. He shall see that the names of all players are entered on the score card, and shall compare his record of the game with that of the opposing second player as each end is declared. At the close of the game he shall hand his score card to his skip.

(d) The lead shall place the mat, and shall deliver the Jack, ensuring that the Jack is properly centred before playing his first bowl.

(e) In addition to the duties specified in the preceding clauses any player may undertake such duties as may be assigned to him by the skip in Clause 52(a) hereof.

RESULT OF END

53. 'The Shot'
A shot or shots shall be adjudged by the bowl or bowls nearer to the Jack than any bowl by the opposing player or players.
When the last bowl has come to rest, half a minute shall elapse if either team desires, before the shots are counted. Neither the Jack or bowls shall be moved until each skip has agreed to the number of shots, except in circumstances where a bowl has to be moved to allow the measuring of another bowl.

54. Measuring conditions to be observed
No measuring shall be allowed until the end has been completed.
All measurements shall be made to the nearest point of each object. If a bowl requiring to be measured is resting on another bowl which prevents its measurement, the best available means shall be taken to secure its position, whereupon the other bowl shall be removed. The same course shall be followed where more than two bowls are involved, or where, in the course of measuring, a single bowl is in danger of falling or otherwise changing its position.
When it is necessary to measure to a bowl or Jack in the ditch, and another bowl or Jack on the green, the measurement shall be made with a flexible measure. Calipers may be used to determine the shot only when the bowls in question and the Jack are on the same plane. The Sonic Measure may be used in all appropriate

circumstances when available.

55. 'Tie' – No Shot

When at the conclusion of play in any end the nearest bowl of each team is touching the Jack, or is deemed to be equidistant from the Jack, there shall be no score recorded. The end shall be declared 'drawn' and shall be counted a played end.

56. Nothing in these Laws shall be deemed to make it mandatory for the last player to play his last bowl in any end, but he shall declare to his opponent or opposing skip his intention to refrain from playing it before the commencement of determining the result of the end and this declaration shall be irrevocable.

GAMES DECISIONS

57. Games played on one occasion

(a) In the case of a single game, team game or a side game played on one occasion or at any stage of an eliminating competition, the winner shall be the player, team or side of players producing at the end of the game the winning number of sets, or the higher total score of shots, or in the case of a 'game of winning ends' a majority of winning ends.

(b) In the case of competitions and/or matches played on a time basis, it shall be the responsibility of the Controlling Body to ensure that Rules are in existence to cover all such competitions and/or matches. The Controlling Body must ensure that such Rules have been brought to the attention of clubs and competitors who are liable to take part in such a match or competition.

58. Tournament games and Games in series

In the case of competitions on a time basis Rules must be made to cover the circumstances of each such competition. In the case of tournament games and games in series the victory decision shall be awarded to the player, team or side of players producing at the end of the tournament or games in series:

(a) the largest number of winning games
or
(b) the highest shots difference in accordance with the regulations governing the tournament or games in series. Points may be used to indicate game successes.

Where points are equal, shots difference will decide the winner. In the event of shots difference being equal then victory will go to the winner of the match involving the players, team or side of players who were level on points and shots difference. Should equality still prevail then Law 59 will become operative.

59. Playing to a finish and possible drawn games

If in an eliminating competition, consisting of a stated or agreed number of ends, it be found, when all the ends have been played, that the scores are equal, an extra end or ends shall be played until a decision has been reached.

The captains or skips shall toss and the winner shall have the right to decide who shall play first. The extra end shall be played from where the previous end was completed and the mat shall be placed in accordance with Law 24. In the case of more than one extra end being required, the captains or skips shall again toss, and the winner shall have the right to decide who shall play first. In the case of an extra end being declared 'dead', the provisions of Law 23(b) shall apply.

DEFAULTS OF PLAYERS IN FOURS PLAY

60. Absentee players in any team or side

(a) In a single fours game, for a trophy, prize or other competitive award, where a club is represented by only one four, each member of such four shall be a bona-fide member of the club. Unless all four players appear and are ready to play at the end of the maximum waiting period of 30 minutes, or should they introduce an ineligible player, then that team shall forfeit the match to the opposing team.

(b) In a domestic fours game if the number of players cannot be accommodated in full teams of four players, three players may play against three players, but shall suffer the deduction of one fourth of the total score of

each team.

A smaller number of players than six shall be excluded from that game.

(c) **In a Side game.** If within a period of 30 minutes from the time fixed for the game, a single player is absent from one or both teams in a side game, whether a friendly club match or a match for a trophy, prize or other award, the game shall proceed, but in the defaulting team, the number of bowls shall be made up by the lead and second players playing three bowls each, but one-fourth of the total shots scored by each 'four' playing three men shall be deducted from their score at the end of the game. Fractions shall be taken into account.

(d) **In a Side game.** Should such default take place where more fours than one are concerned, or where a four has been disqualified for some other infringement, and where the average score is to decide the contest, the scores of the non-defaulting fours only shall be counted, but such average shall, as a penalty in the case of the defaulting side, be arrived at by dividing the aggregate score of that side by the number of fours that should have been played and not as in the case of the other side, by the number actually engaged in the game.

61. Play Irregularities

(a) **Playing out of turn.** When a player has played before his turn, the opposing skip shall have the right to stop the bowl in its course, and it shall be played in its proper turn, but in the event of the bowl so played having disturbed any part of the head, the opposing skip shall have the option of allowing the head to remain as it is after the bowl so played has come to rest, or having the end declared 'dead'.

(b) **Playing the wrong bowl.** A bowl played by mistake shall be replaced by the player's own bowl.

(c) **Changing bowls.** A player shall not be allowed to change his bowls during the course of a game, or in a resumed game, unless they be objected to as provided in Law 9(c), or when a bowl has been so damaged in the course of play as, in the opinion of the Umpire, to render the bowl (or bowls) unfit for play.

(d) **Omitting to play**
(1) If the result of an end has been agreed upon, or the head has been touched in the agreed process of determining the result, then a player who forfeits or has omitted to play a bowl, shall forfeit the right to play it.

(2) A player who has neglected to play a bowl in the proper sequence shall forfeit the right to play such a bowl if a bowl has been played by each team before such mistake was discovered.

(3) If, before the mistake be noticed, a bowl has been delivered in the reversed order and the head has not been disturbed, the opponent shall then play two successive bowls to restore the correct sequence.
If the head has been disturbed, Clause 61(a) shall apply.

62. Play Interruptions

(a) **Game Stoppages.** When a game of any kind is stopped, either by mutual arrangement or by the Umpire, after appeal to him on account of darkness or any other valid reason, it shall be resumed with the scores as they were when the game stopped. An end commenced, but not completed, shall be declared null and void.

(b) **Substitutes in a resumed game.** If in a resumed game any one of the four original players be not available, one substitute shall be permitted as stated in Law 63 below. Players however, shall not be transferred from one team to another.

INFLUENCES AFFECTING PLAY

63. Leaving the Green

If during the course of a side, fours, triples or pairs game a player has to leave the green owing to illness, or other reasonable cause, his place shall be filled by a substitute, if in the opinion of

both skips (or failing agreement by them, then in the opinion of the Controlling Body) such substitution is necessary. Should the player affected be a skip, his duties and position in a fours game shall be assumed by the third player, and the substitute shall play either as a lead, second or third. In the case of triples the substitute may play either as lead or second but not as skip and in the case of pairs the substitute may play as lead only. Such substitute shall be a member of the club to which the team belongs. In domestic play National Associations may decide the position of any substitute. If during the course of a single-handed game, a player has to leave the green owing to illness, or reasonable cause, the provision of Law 62(a) shall be observed.

No player shall be allowed to delay the play by leaving the rink or team, unless with the consent of his opponent, and then only for a period not exceeding ten minutes.

Contravention of this Law shall entitle the opponent or opposing team to claim the game or match.

64. Objects on the Green

Under no circumstances, other than provided in Laws 5, 29, 33 and 40, shall any extraneous object to assist a player be placed on the green or on the bank, or on the Jack, or on a bowl elsewhere.

65. Unforeseen incidents

If during the course of play, the position of the Jack or bowls be disturbed by any neutral object the end shall be declared 'dead' unless the skips are agreed as to the replacement of Jacks or bowls.

DOMESTIC ARRANGEMENTS

66. In addition to any matters specifically mentioned in these Laws, a Member Governing Body may, in circumstances dictated by local conditions (and with the approval of the World Indoor Bowls Council, where this is appropriate), make such other Regulations as are deemed necessary and desirable. For this purpose the Member Governing Body shall appoint a committee to be known as the 'Laws Committee' with power to grant approval or otherwise to any proposal, with such decision being valid until the proposal is submitted to the World Indoor Bowls Council for final decision.

67. Local Arrangements

Affiliated or member clubs shall, in making their local arrangements, make such regulations as are deemed necessary to govern their club competitions; but such regulations shall be approved by the National Governing Body and be displayed.

68. National Visiting Teams or Sides

No team or side of bowlers visiting another country shall be recognised by the World Indoor Bowls Council, unless it is first sanctioned and recommended by the Member Governing Body, to which its members are affiliated.

69. Contracting Out

No Club or Club Management Committee or any individual shall have the right or power to contract out of any of the Laws of the Game governing Indoor Bowls as laid down by the World Indoor Bowls Council.

REGULATING SINGLE-HANDED, PAIRS AND TRIPLES GAME

70. The foregoing Laws, where applicable, shall also apply to single-handed, pairs and triples games.

SPECTATORS

71. Persons not engaged in the game shall be situated clear of and beyond the limits of the rink of play, and clear of the banks. They shall neither by word nor act disturb or advise the players. The second sentence does not apply in respect of the advice given from beyond the bank by a non- playing Captain or Manager of the team or side. The setting up of betting stands on the premises of affiliated clubs in connection with any game or games shall not

be permitted.

DUTIES OF MARKER

72.
(a) In the absence of the Umpire the Marker shall control the game in accordance with the Laws of the Game governing Indoor Bowls as approved by the World Indoor Bowls Council.
(b) He shall centre the Jack and place a full length Jack in compliance with Law 29.
(c) He shall ensure that the Jack is not less than 75 feet (22.86 metres) from the centre of the front edge of the mat to comply with Law 30.
(d) He shall stand at one side of the rink, and to the rear of the Jack. The position of the Marker may be affected by television cameras.
(e) He shall answer concisely any enquiry by a player.
(f) Subject to contrary instructions from either opponent under Law 34 he shall mark all 'touchers' immediately they come to rest, and remove chalk marks from 'non-touchers'. With the agreement of both opponents he shall remove all 'dead' bowls from the green and the ditch. He shall mark the positions of the Jack and 'touchers' which are in the ditch (See Laws 33 and 40).
(g) He shall not move or cause to be moved either the Jack or bowls until each player has agreed to the number of shots.
(h) He shall measure carefully all doubtful shots when requested to do so by either player. He shall ask the players to remove from the head all bowls which are not involved in the measure.
If unable to come to a decision acceptable to the players he shall call on an Umpire. If an official Umpire has not been appointed, the Marker shall select one. The decision of the Umpire shall be final.
The World Indoor Bowls Council, The British Isles Indoor Bowls Council and Member Governing Bodies reserve the right to amend the Duties of a Marker to suit special circumstances.
(i) He shall enter the score at each end and intimate to the players the state of the game. When the game is finished he shall see that the score card containing the name of the players is signed by the players and disposed of in accordance with the Rules of the Competition
(j) The Marker may indicate verbally or by signal, his opinion of the shot or shots as unobtrusively as possible. The method of indication must not disturb the concentration of the players in any way.

DUTIES OF UMPIRE

73. An Umpire shall be appointed by the appropiated Controlling Body. His duties shall be as follows:
(a) He shall examine all bowls for the imprint of the I.B.B. Stamp, and ascertain by measurement the width of the rinks of play.
(b) He shall measure any shot or shots in dispute, and for this purpose shall use a suitable measure. His decision shall be final.
(c) He shall decide all questions as to the distance of the mat from the ditch, and the Jack from the mat.
(d) He shall decide as to whether or not the Jack and/or bowls are in play.
(e) He shall enforce the Laws of the Game.
(f) In Championships and International Matches the Umpires decision shall be final in respect of any breach of a Law, except that, upon questions relating to the meaning or interpretation of any Law, there shall be a right of appeal to the Controlling Body.
(g) The World Indoor Bowls Council, The British Isles Indoor Bowls Council and Member Governing Bodies reserve the right to amend duties of an Umpire to suit special circumstances.
(h) Permissable variations for televised events. Assisting Umpires may be appointed who shall aid the Umpire as required.

WORLD INDOOR BOWLS COUNCIL BY-LAWS

Players' Status
All players considered to have amateur status, except those players whose principal source of income is derived fom *playing* the game of bowls.

Stamping of Bowls
Each bowl complying with the requirements of Law 9 shall be stamped with the registered stamp of the International Bowling Board.

Stamping of Bowls
Manufacturers will be entitled to use the registered I.B.B. stamp to facilitate the imprint between the inner an outer rings of bowls. Imprints on running surfaces should be avoided wherever possible.

Stamp Details

B.B.	International Bowling Board.
A	Denotes factory of manufacture
Numerals	Denotes year of expiry
®	Trademark

Metric Equivalent (Composition Bowls)
In connection with the manufacture of bowls there is no objection to manufacturers using metric equivalents in lieu of the present figures, always provided that Law 9 is complied with. Furthermore, there is no objection to manufacturers indicating various sizes of bowls by numerals and the manufacturers will be entitled to use the following table if they so desire.

Size in Inches	Size Number	Actual Metric (mm)	May be rounded off Metric (mm)
4.5/8	0	117.4	117
4.3/4	1	120.7	121
4.13/16	2	122.2	122
4.7/8	3	123.8	124
4.15/16	4	125.4	125
5	5	127.0	127
5.1/16	6	128.6	129
5.1/8	7	130.2	130

If size numbers are utilised and size measurements omitted then no bowl in diameter shall be less than 4⅝ inches (117.4 mm) nor more than 5⅛ inches (130.2 mm) and no bowl shall weigh more than 3 lb 8 oz (1.59 kg).

CODE OF PRACTICE FOR INDOOR GREENS
This Code of Practice has been introduced to cover items formerly within the Laws of the Game, but which vary slightly within each of the countries in membership of the World Indoor Bowls Council.

APPLICATION WITHIN ENGLAND – THE GREEN

2. The Green – Area and Surfaces
The green shall form a rectangle or square of not less than 105 feet (32 metres) and not more than 132 feet (40.23 metres) long with a width of not less than 15 feet (4.57 metres). It shall have a suitable playing surface which shall be level. The ends shall be provided with suitable boundaries in the form of a ditch and bank.

3. The Ditch
The two end ditches shall have a holding surface not injurious to bowls and shall be free from obstacles. The ditch shall be not less than 8 inches (203 mm) nor more than 15 inches (381 mm) wide, and it shall not less than 2 inches (51 mm) nor more than 8 inches (203 mm) below the level of the green.
Ditches should also be supplied on the long side of the green, although this is not essential as indoor greens are only used in one direction. If

the land available is limited the side boundaries may be supplied by wooden slats or boards or by a wall suitably cushioned so that bowls do not receive any damage on impact.

4. Banks
The banks shall be not less than 9 inches (229 mm) above the level of the green. The surface of the banks shall not be injurious to bowls.

APPLICATION WITHIN IRELAND

All affiliated clubs must have their own Indoor Green with a playing surface of not less than 114 feet (34.75 metres) or more than 132 feet (40.23 metres) in length, and each rink must be not less than 14 feet (4.27 metres) in width. Outside rinks must have an extra 18 inches (46 cm) of playing surface beyond the outside boundary of the rink. There must be banks and ditches at each end of the Indoor Green as specified in the By-Laws made under the W.I.B.C. Laws of the Game governing Indoor Bowls. Only clubs with a minimum of 4 rinks, and complying with the fore-going conditions can be considered for affiliation.

APPLICATION WITHIN SCOTLAND

A specification covering the dimensions of a new Indoor Green in Scotland has been prepared by the Honorary Architect to the S.I.B.A.. Full details can be obtained from the Honorary Secretary of the Association whose address is contained within the current S.I.B.A. Year Book. Clubs with two or three rinks of satisfactory dimensions are eligible to apply for Restricted Membership of the Association only, whilst clubs with a minumum of four rinks can apply for Full Membership of the Association. Full details of membership conditions are contained within the current S.I.B.A. Year Book.

APPLICATION WITHIN WALES

The Indoor Green shall have a playing surface of at least 105 feet (32 metres) in length and each rink a minumum of 14 feet (4.27 metres) in width with banks and ditches at each end. Only clubs with a minumum of two rinks which comply with the previously mentioned specification shall be considered for affiliation. New clubs are recommended to lay down an Indoor Green having a minumum of four rinks, each being a minumum length of 114 feet (34.75 metres) and a minimum width of 15 feet (4.57 metres) with banks and ditches at both ends. Details of the specification to cover all aspects of a new indoor green in Wales can be obtained by contacting the Honorary Secretary of the Welsh Indoor Bowls Association.

TONY ALLCOCK: A PEN PORTRAIT

Born in Thurmaston, Leicestershire, on the 11th June, 1955, Tony Allcock was an early bowls enthusiast, influenced by his late mother, Joan, who bowled for England, and his father, Ernie, who was a county player. Tony was born, he boasts, between two rounds of the club pairs competition, which his mother went on to win. No wonder he describes himself as 'a natural born bowler'.

He took up many other pursuits, however, including riding ponies and entering gymkhanas (Quorn Pony Club). He owned two ponies, and also bred and judged pedigree rabbits and cavies. Another early taste of competition was as a singer, his fine treble voice earning him titles at Leicester, Tamworth, Kettering and Derby.

He 'returned' to bowls at 14, joining the local village club at Fosseway, Syston, Leicestershire, because the top clubs he approached considered him too young. He persuaded his school friend, Paul Clarke, to join with him, and together they won their first county title – the pairs – in 1972. At 17, Allcock and Clarke duly made their first appearances at the EBA national championships, then played at the famous Watneys Sports Ground, Mortlake.

Success followed success as Tony went on to win England's Under 25 singles title in 1975, aged 20, a feat which he repeated two years later. In 1976, three months before his 21st birthday, he represented England in the indoor international series at Rugby Thornfield – and was promoted to skip for the third game, against Scotland. His first outdoor cap arrived in 1978.

In 1980, with Jimmy Hobday and David Bryant, Allcock won his first World title, when he played as the middle man in the English triple. He regards Bryant as the greatest bowler who has ever lived, and his association with the Clevedon Maestro has continued to be a successful one. Together they have twice won the Midland Bank World indoor pairs title, and twice been runners up in the World outdoor pairs – at Aberdeen in 1984, and at Auckland in 1988.

The World outdoor fours title came Tony's way in 1984, and he has consolidated his position as arguably the world's currently most successful player by winning the Embassy World indoor singles twice in succession (in 1986 and 1987) and bagging five English indoor titles in four winters: singles twice (1985 and 1987); triples twice (1986 and 1988); fours once (1986).

Tony was the *McCarthy & Stone* and *Daily Telegraph* Player of the Year in 1987, and has been four times voted Player of the Year by readers of the monthly magazine, *Bowls International*, from 1985 to 1988 inclusive.

Until August, 1987, he was Principal of an Adult Training Centre for the Mentally Handicapped in Stroud, where he was a dedicated member of a caring profession. His decision to leave his vocation for a full-time career in bowls was a difficult one to take – but, although he has now formed his own company, he still finds time to be Chairman of the Gloucestershire Special Olympics committee, and Patron of the English Visually Handicapped Bowling Association.

Tony Allcock now lives in the historic Worcestershire village of Broadway, but he continues to play bowls for the Cheltenham club in the spa town's picturesque Suffolk Square. Indoors, he plays from the Cotswold club at Stroud. He likes to relax by studying, collecting antiques, and listening to music – especially opera.

TONY ALLCOCK'S RECORD

OUTDOOR.

WORLD BOWLS CHAMPIONSHIPS:

PAIRS – 1984 silver; 1988 silver;
TRIPLES – 1980 gold;
FOURS – 1984 gold; 1988 bronze;
LEONARD TROPHY – 1980 gold; 1988 gold.

ENGLISH BOWLING ASSOCIATION NATIONAL CHAMPIONSHIPS:

SINGLES – Runner up 1987.

UNDER 25 SINGLES – Winner 1975, 77, 81; Runner up 1974.

COUNTY TOP FOUR – Winner 1982; Runner up 1985.

AUSTRALIAN MAZDA INTERNATIONAL INVITATION EVENT:

SINGLES – 1985 silver.

INDOOR.

EMBASSY WORLD SINGLES CHAMPIONSHIP:

Winner 1986, 87.

MIDLAND BANK WORLD PAIRS CHAMPIONSHIP:

Winner 1986, 87.

BRITISH ISLES SINGLES CHAMPIONSHIP:
Winner 1988.

CROFT ORIGINAL BRITISH OPEN SINGLES CHAMPIONSHIP:

Winner 1985.

CIS UK SINGLES CHAMPIONSHIP:

Winner 1987; Runner up 1984.

ENGLISH INDOOR BOWLING ASSOCIATION NATIONAL CHAMPIONSHIPS:

SINGLES – Winner 1985, 87.
UNDER 31 SINGLES – Winner 1984.
CHAMPION OF CHAMPIONS SINGLES –
Winner 1983.
TRIPLES – Winner 1986, 88.
FOURS – Winner 1986.

WELSH TENNANTS LAGER CLASSIC:

Winner 1985.

IRISH INDOOR MASTERS:

Winner 1986.

CIS INTERNATIONAL MIXED PAIRS CHAMPIONSHIP:

Winner 1987, 88.

INDEX